TELLING
LIVES

TELLING
LIVES THE
BIOGRAPHER'S ART

Edited by
MARC PACHTER

University of Pennsylvania Press   1981

by
LEON EDEL
JUSTIN KAPLAN
ALFRED KAZIN
DORIS KEARNS
THEODORE ROSENGARTEN
BARBARA W. TUCHMAN
GEOFFREY WOLFF

Hardcover edition published by New Republic Books,
Washington, D.C.

Paperback edition published in 1981 by the
University of Pennsylvania Press, Philadelphia,
by arrangement with New Republic Books.

Library of Congress Cataloging in Publication Data

Main entry under title:

Telling lives, the biographer's art.

   Originally published: Washington: New Republic
Books, 1979.
   Contents: The biographer himself/Marc Pachter
—The figure under the carpet/Leon Edel—The
naked self and other problems/Justin Kaplan—
[etc.]
   1.   Biography (as a literary form)—Addresses,
essays, lectures.   I.   Edel, Leon, 1907–
II.   Pachter, Marc.
[CT21.T44   1981]   808'.06692021   81-10312

ISBN 0-8122-1118-9 (pbk.)   AACR2

Printed in the United States of America

 For Lisa

Acknowledgments

An editor only provides a forum for his contributors. The book is truly theirs, and I am very grateful to these seven distinguished writers for their forceful and eloquent essays.

Telling Lives had its origins in a symposium on biography that took place at the National Portrait Gallery, Smithsonian Institution. Marvin Sadik, director of the Gallery, is responsible, through his support and counsel, not only for the success of the symposium itself but for the comprehensive vision of a portrait gallery underlying it. The transformation of symposium into book, which began through the good offices of Jack Beatty, literary editor of *The New Republic* magazine, was shaped by Joan Tapper, editorial director of New Republic Books, who added three essays to the original four and became through the months of our collaboration not only a colleague but a friend. We both depended greatly on Fran Moshos to shepherd the book through its various stages.

Within my office at the National Portrait Gallery, Eloise Harvey typed transcripts, manuscripts, and letters with her usual, wondrous equanimity, and Amy Henderson, assistant historian, and Jeannette Hussey, research historian, proved again how much I can count on them for advice and help.

Contents

TELLING LIVES

MARC PACHTER
The Biographer Himself:
An Introduction

"We do not reflect that it is perhaps as difficult to write a good life as to live one."

Lytton Strachey

"**I**s it not curious," remarked André Maurois in the historic series of lectures on "Aspects of Biography," which he delivered at Trinity College, Cambridge University, "how the metaphor of the portrait painter crops up as soon as one begins to talk of the biographer?" Fifty years later the National Portrait Gallery took note of that special bond and convened in Washington, D.C., during its tenth anniversary celebration, an unprecedented gathering of biographers. They were all—in the metaphor of the occasion—verbal portraitists, these biographers of Jefferson, Mary Cassatt, and Dos Passos, of Dulles, Mencken, and Whistler—who had come together to hear Leon Edel, Doris Kearns, Justin Kaplan, and Barbara Tuchman discuss the art of telling lives. This book, expanded to include other voices from the community of life writers, is a tribute to the vitality of their art.

Distinguished biography, as defined in the following essays, bears no resemblance to the voluminous, indiscriminate compendia of facts-shoveled-on-facts in which the biographer buries alive both his hero and the reader. At the heart of great biography is selectivity, keyed, in Professor

Edel's phrase, to "the essence of a life." The eye of the fine biographer, like that of the portrait painter, sculptor, or photographer, catches the special gleam of character. Through him, we encounter another human being, we feel the presence of a recognizable, approachable life.

But the biographer's achievement is hard won. Inundated by thousands of documents and impressions ("Sorted till I was stupefied," wrote Boswell in 1786), or starved for the lack of them; embraced by the subject, his family, friends, and disciples, or waylaid by them at every turn, the biographer must somehow deliver a convincing life. What sustains him is the near-missionary drive to save, if not a soul then a personality for the company of future generations. "The more I learned about Oliver Wendell Holmes," wrote Catherine Drinker Bowen in her *Adventures of a Biographer* (1959), "the more insupportable it became to think of him as dead, cold and motionless beneath that stone at Arlington. I found myself possessed by a witch's frenzy to ungrave this man, stand him upright, see him walk, jump, dance, tell jokes, make love, display his vanity or his courage as the case might be. National encomium, the laying on of laurels, had only buried him deeper. The difficulty was to uncover material that gave proof of life—not noble public posture but characteristic brief turns of phrase, small oddities and manners that belonged to Holmes and Holmes alone."

Not everyone, of course, wants to see the great "walk, jump," and "dance," or to discover their human needs and limitations. To those who prefer their heroes on pedestals, the biographer's pursuit of personality is iconoclasm—the impulse, snapped the Victorian writer John Morley, "to contemplate the hinder parts of their divinities." Certainly there are those who write biographies to diminish their subjects, clear gestures of spite that do find an audience, but the biographer's search for what Bowen called "material that gives the proof of life" is not negative in intent and rarely in effect. It is based on the conviction that biographical tributes that are lies in what they say or do not say, one-dimensional portrayals that describe a man who never walked among men, are poor tributes and worse art. If we learn, for example, that George Washington had large feet—and he had, the marvel of his age—we are not edified, but we are warmed to the presence of a living being; we are less worshipful and more intrigued. The idealizing biography, like the standard boardroom portrait and other totems of respectability, begs to be ignored. Unwilling to genuflect before his subject, the biographer pulls him back into his humanity. Boswell, reports the literary historian Richard Altrick, when asked by Dr. Samuel Johnson's friend, Hannah More, to soften his portrayal of the "asperities . . . (of) our virtuous and most revered departed friend," replied that "he would not cut off his claws, nor make a tiger a cat, to please anybody."

His commitment to candid portrayal can earn the biographer far worse than the antagonism of the reverent. He demands access to every aspect of his subject's life, and the subject, contemplating his biographer, born or unborn, rebels. The field of literary history is thick with the smoke of burning letters: Dickens's batch of twenty years in one famous case, Henry James's of near-forty years in another. Less dramatically, T.S. Eliot chose to add a simple codicil to his will: "I do not wish my executors to facilitate or countenance the writing of a biography of me." Even Walt Whitman, who enjoined his "Boswell," Horace Traubel, to "be sure to write about me honest; whatever you do, do not prettify me: include all the hells and damns," even Whitman we learn, sorted, falsified, and burned.

One can understand this instinct for self-protection, the reluctance to share one's intimate life with some unknown representative of posterity—pinned by him like a butterfly to a board. The spectacle of writers destroying the revealing evidence of their lives outrages our historical sensibilities but engages our human sympathy. The issue of privacy has to be raised: What right has the biographer to pursue his subject to the privatemost corners of his life? Must a writer's work, or that of any other public figure, open him up to unending scrutiny? "What business has the public to know about Byron's wildnesses?" demanded Tennyson. "He has given them fine work and they ought to be satisfied." And in our own century, W.H. Auden, quoted here by Geoffrey Wolff, insists for all writers that *"our* sufferings, *our* weaknesses are of no literary interest whatsoever."

But the biographer, even the compassionate biographer, knowing his subject's resentment, his dread, his disdain for what biographers cannot know, nonetheless persists. He does so not because he believes that one must know a life to appreciate the meaning of its artistic work. Biographers do not aspire to literary criticism. Their approach is exactly the reverse, searching the work for clues to the life. But by what right do they search at all? Public lives are not lived in isolation; they have impact far beyond their immediate circle and therefore invite a response. If certain lives have the power to touch or to transform our own (quite literally, in the case of the political world), to exalt or to terrify us, then we, with the biographer as our representative, have the right to make sense of those lives, to their innermost nature.

This, however, is only moral auditing—the balancing of the legitimate rights of history against those of the individual—and biographers rarely engage in it. What they do claim, with certainty, is not their right but their need to know—a need they share with their large audience. Interest in other people, and particularly in those who have accomplished a great deal, would seem to be fundamental to our nature. And even those who are marked men, as Ernest Samuels described Henry Adams, are often themselves, like Adams, voracious readers of the biographies and auto-biographies of other people's lives. (Adams, Samuels explains, understood that biographers have an obligation to tell the whole truth about a life. "The trouble is," wrote Adams, "that any truthful biography must always define the hero's limitations." He saw his own autobiography as "a shield of protection in the grave.") W.H. Auden, according to his literary executor, Edward Mendelson, made a number of exceptions to his profound dislike of the principle of artistic biography when he found the story of a particular life "absolutely fascinating," as with Wagner, Trollope, and Pope. And Henry James, too, who thwarted his unborn biographer at every turn, was a reader (and a writer) of personal histories, and even set down the guiding rule that "To live over other people's lives is nothing unless we live over their perceptions, live over the growth the change the varying intensity of the same—since it was by these things they themselves lived."

The biographer's drive is our human curiosity made intense and particular. His is a "passion for life," in Harold Nicolson's phrase, a will to know the true shape of another's experience, to capture it in the face of all resistance. Unsqueamish on this issue, he accepts the adversary relationship. "One can't blame these fugitives," writes Justin Kaplan, "they know that even the best disposed biographers have to have an inquisitorial aspect if they are to arrive at any sort of truth." His search for the truth in a life, then, is the biographer's preeminent standard, and his own response to that truth shapes his art. How far he probes, what he chooses to reveal, is determined not by his subject's sensibilities but by the personal instincts and affinities that lead him to take hold. It is only when he fails to respond fully, when he undertakes a biography in a spirit of obligation to greatness, collecting and categorizing its droppings for the sake of posterity, that he truly betrays that life by robbing it of its vitality, and produces one of those vast, mournful compendia that add, someone once said, a new terror to dying.

It is easy to lose sight of the biographer's formative role. Looking principally at the greatness of the life-subject itself, one can miss the book's central, its shaping temperament. When the life is "minor" in its range and in its creative work,

Harry Crosby's, for example, as portrayed by Geoffrey Wolff, reviewers are perplexed to find themselves moved by an insignificant life, and are unable to accept—as they would naturally do in a novel or a play—the author's own commitment and narrative power as the measure of the book's validity and its artistry. When the life is great, and therefore "legitimate" as a subject, the biographer, and particularly the biographer who has done his work well, vanishes into the shadow of his creative achievement, and critical attention centers on what appears to be *the* life of Theodore Roosevelt, or Benjamin Franklin, or of Margaret Fuller rather than on *a* life seen, in Edel's words, "through particular eyes."

Still, if the biographer is *there* in his work, he is only there in a certain way, which is difficult to define. The greater his skill, the finer his intuition of personality, the less aware we are of him in our experience of the narrated life. This is not inevitably so. If he is a master of irony, like Lytton Strachey at work on the Victorians, he can make his presence and mordant humor known through sly juxtaposition and telling revelations, and get away with it. Few do. If he personally knew the subject, he can legitimately enter the life drama as a principal character, although Professor Edel would argue that what emerges is a memoir and not a true biography. Or if, like Geoffrey Wolff and Theodore Rosengarten, he not only portrays but seizes a life from obscurity, he can emerge more explicitly as its "sponsor." But even allowing for those exceptions (and putting aside for a moment the greatest exception of all, the telling of one's own life), the biographer must avoid center stage. He commits, often unintentionally, the one unforgivable sin if he violates the spirit of the life by intruding his theories upon its meaning. "The challenge," writes Doris Kearns, "is to ask the right question, not merely the one satisfactory to oneself." Drawn to his subject by an affinity and a fascination that he may not always fully comprehend, the biographer must not allow the life to become a vehicle for the airing of his biases, or, worse, for the satisfaction of his own longings, distorting the life to prove a point emotionally necessary to himself.

One ironic sequence in the history of American biography shows the danger. Asked to do a life of Nathaniel Hawthorne for an American authors series, Henry James, settled by then into an agreeable and nourishing cosmopolitanism, set a trap for his subject. James produced a diminished Hawthorne to prove his thesis that no American writer could develop fully in the arid soil of his native land. Like his protagonist in "The Jolly Corner," returned from an extended stay abroad, James saw, in Hawthorne, the ghost of himself as he might have been. Then, in a twist of circumstance, James's career became itself the occasion for a biographer to rehearse his anxieties. Van Wyck Brooks, lapsed esthete and spokesman for American cultural nationalism in the early twentieth century, wrote his life of the master expatriate as a tale of wasted promise—portraying James as a writer cast adrift on a sea of literary exoticism. Like the biography of Hawthorne before it, Brooks's *The Pilgrimage of Henry James* (1925) was less a life than the exploitation of a life.

Balance can also be upset, conversely, when the biographer loses himself in his subject. To identify too closely with a life, to collapse into adulation, is to give up the distance that allows the writer to become something more than the agent for a reputation. One can fall into the role willingly, as in the authorized biography where objectivity may be qualified for the sake of the cooperation of family and friends and of access to restricted materials. But more often it is the force of the subject's personality, its power to fascinate or to dominate, which binds the biographer. The threat is all the greater when biographer and subject know each other. With allowance for Boswell, Edel wonders if valid biography is even possible under such circumstances. Kearns and Wolff, analyzing their own subjectivity—in the portrayal of an employer in her case and a father in his—believe balance can be achieved; but the Boswellian biographer walks on eggshells.

The major struggle between writer and subject is fought here, in the arena of reputation. A modern biographer may or may not choose to reveal the intimate, the amorous details of a life, but he must, if he is good at what he does, probe beneath its public, polished self. The doubts and vulnerabilities, the meannesses, ambitions, and private satisfactions that are hidden within a social personality yield him his greatest insights. Seeking to reveal what his subject filters out as unworthy or perhaps only as uninteresting, he becomes for him, we have seen, an adversary to be frustrated, coopted, or even out-smarted ("It will read charmingly in your biography," Jane Carlyle wrote bitingly of an insincere letter from her husband). A life taken only at its own crafted word is imperfectly and even unjustly rendered. Fine biography challenges the pose to find the personality.

Admittedly, this is a modern notion. Throughout much of the last century, the biographer saw his task as testimonial: the narration of a great public life. An ally of reputation and even of legend, he extended its sway to posterity. The nineteenth-century biographer's vantage point—the heights of Olympus—seems, of course, rather less gorgeous today. We find it hard to accept the likes of Parson Mason Locke Weems, celebrant of the boy Washington in the drama of the cherry tree. But we too easily miss the integrity of the heroic, the exemplary biography. What seems to us hypocrisy was in fact the expression of a coherent world view, which judged the inner, the more familiar life—the life, so to speak, outside history and fixed morality—as far less authentic a standard for meaning. The convincing life was the life of record, of inspiration, of action. While this suited the code of gentility, it was not shaped to serve its purposes. Man's private nature was just that; to explore it was a diversion—a *low* diversion— from the fundamental drama.

The early nineteenth century could see, as we cannot, a comfortable equation of personal and social history. Ralph Waldo Emerson pronounced for his era: "There is properly no history: only biography." And if biography was history itself, it was only biography ennobled, selected from the moral and public highlights of a life to shape a sense of the age. "The history of mankind," wrote Carlyle, "is the history of its great men: to find out these, clean the dirt from them, and place them on their proper pedestals." The belief that man could control events was a wedge of secular optimism thrust between the traditional view of the divine role in history, and our own sense of the impersonality of society. For a time, as Alfred Kazin says, man was at one with history. And the greatest of men, made heroic not only by their efforts but by the worship of them as heroes (as in Carlyle's philosophical handbook, *On Heroes, Hero-Worship, and the Heroic in History*), were given over to the biographer-priests.

The first serious cracks in the temple appeared some years before Lytton Strachey of Bloomsbury brought it down in our own time. Occasional references to the personality traits and private lives of the great subjects had appeared even in the heyday of heroic biography (particularly when such notorious figures as Lord Byron refused their pedestals), but a significant shift in emphasis, alarming to the reverent, began to be felt in the last decades of the century. Ironically, it was Thomas Carlyle, as subject this time rather than as author, who straddled the divide. James Anthony Froude undertook to write the life of the sage, in Daniel Aaron's words, "as a sacred obligation," and would certainly not seem by our standards a despoiler of heroism. But Froude laced his epic four-volume account (based on his seventeen-year close friendship from 1864 to 1881), with powerful vignettes of the raging Carlyle personality, and candid reports of the domestic snakepit he shared with his extraordinary wife and well-matched opponent Jane. The scandal nearly buried Froude under a mound of abuse, but he survived, as rather a heroic figure himself to his fellow biographers.

The growing interest in the nonpublic sphere of personality had precedents that reached far back beyond the Victorian mode. Plutarch, as near a patron saint as biographers have, wrote, in his *Life of Alexander*: "It must be borne in mind that my purpose is not to write histories, but lives. . . . Sometimes . . . an expression or a jest informs us better of their characteristics and inclinations, than the most famous sieges, the greatest armaments or the bloodiest battles whatsoever. Therefore as portrait-painters are more exact in the forms and features of the face, in which the character is seen, than in the other parts of the body, so I must be allowed to give my more particular attention to the marks and indications of the souls of men." Plutarch's separation of "histories" and "lives" had meaning for a new generation fascinated by the unique, even idiosyncratic qualities of men and women: their human temperament. This reawakened sense of what was compelling in a life was encouraged by a growing disenchantment with the possibilities of heroism in a world seen as increasingly impersonal, and a growing impatience, too, with the hammerlock hold of gentility. The public career no longer seemed self-sufficient as the central drama in a life, the private sphere no longer seemed dismissable as the shameful or merely trivial domain of the personality.

What was suppressed before in the interest of ethical or historical coherence became therefore, by the early twentieth century, the very rough-edged core of biography. In the age of Freud, biographers used psychological insights to turn marble into flesh, and sometimes into weak flesh. Life-writing, in the aftermath of Victorianism, took on some of the aspects of exposé. It was a period of antiheroism, of the destruction of the public myth. At his least pleasant, the new biographer was a smug practitioner of oneupsmanship, who bled a life dry of its vitality and authority. But when the biographer was a master, like Lytton Strachey, he presented a remarkable and vivid character to savor even in its limitations. It was with Strachey that biography saw again its possibilities as an evocative literary form. His preface to *Eminent Victorians* (1918) served as its declaration of independence from Victorian ritual:

> Those two fat volumes, with which it is our custom to commemorate the dead—who does not know them—with their ill-digested masses of material, their slipshod style, their tone of tedious panegyric, their lamentable lack of selection, of detachment, of design? They are as familiar as the *cortege* of the undertaker, and wear the same air of slow, funereal barbarism. One is tempted to suppose, of some of them, that they have been composed by that functionary, as the final item of his job. . . . How many lessons are to be learned from them. . . . To preserve, for instance, a becoming brevity—a brevity which excludes everything that is redundant and nothing that is significant—that, surely, is the first duty of the biographer. The second, no less surely, is to maintain his own freedom of spirit. It is not his business to be complimentary, it is his business to lay bare the facts of the case as he understands them.

What biography has become since the early twentieth century can be seen in the following essays. There has been no abandonment of the ideals of brevity or of honest evocation of the truth in a life; but there has been some change in the understanding of what that truth may be. Modern biographers are far less likely to "expose" a life, to treat its public ideals and manners, its perfected sense of self, as an ironic backdrop to the true inner drama of character. The biographer is less the judge or debunker: He is far more willing to accept as valid and revealing, if not as literally true, an individual's improved presentation of himself before the world. His goal is to portray, as Justin Kaplan has written, "the whole sense of a person," the relationship between the public ideal of himself, which he holds as his "personal mythology," and the inner fears, longings, and spirited aspirations that call it forth.

To comprehend the dynamic in a personality—its evolving sense of itself as it is and as it would like to be—the biographer first uncovers the truth. In his brief discussion of Henry David Thoreau, Leon Edel cautions us not to take too literally the pose of isolation at Walden Pond, but to recognize, as well, its mythic power as the organizing principle in Thoreau's personality and his art. Doris Kearns's revealing account of her efforts to sort out Lyndon Johnson's impressions of his origins suggests, again, how much can be learned about an individual from the facts he invents about himself.

The biographer, therefore, probes in sympathy—to define the myth that orders his subject's experience and that offers the key to his nature. He is a collaborator in the creation of meaning in a life, taking upon himself its most fundamental concerns. Justin Kaplan, who discusses here his study of Walt Whitman, writes of "the biographer's obligation to give Whitman himself the freedom he never had to pursue his recognition that love, of whatever sort it may be, was the root of roots in his life and poetry." Geoffrey Wolff states his intentions simply: *"Here's what Harry Crosby did; let me try to show why."* And Theodore Rosengarten's sensitive reading of the uses to which Ned Cobb (Nate Shaw in *All God's Dangers*) put the telling of his own life during months of interviews makes clear how complete is the collaboration in "oral biography." When the life told is one's own, biography becomes itself a crucible of the life myth. "For the nonfiction writer, as I can testify," writes Alfred Kazin, "personal history is directly an effort to find salvation, to make one's own experience come out right."

Life-telling, then, has become an intimate act. The biographer, once content with the public events in a life, wrestles now with its private meaning: Hemingway's anxious masculinity, for example, or Mark Twain's black moods, or Whitman's explosive but perhaps never physically expressed sensuality. The skeptic may well ask how a biographer can truly know a life to this extent. A public career can be mapped, but can the inner development of a personality, both at conscious and subconscious levels? The answer, necessarily, is incomplete. The biographer concedes the problems he faces—the limitations of the materials at hand, the traps set for him, the confusions of psychological theory—but he relies, in the end, on his intuitive ability to create out of the clues he uncovers a convincing vision of a life.

LEON EDEL
The Figure Under the Carpet

A portrait gallery—a national portrait gallery—evokes great pages of history, the distant and the near past. It is an exhilarating experience to come upon faces of characters one has known only in history books. I remember a particular thrill of my youth when I wandered into the rooms of Britain's National Portrait Gallery housing the eminent Victorians— so eminent, so assured, so rubicund, so gouty, so marked in feature and countenance. At that moment I crossed a magical threshold of the past. I was at large in the nineteenth century with Spencer and Huxley, Darwin and Green, Gladstone and Disraeli. Equally thrilling was the experience of finding myself among writers all the way back to the Romantics— Byron, sexy and sultry in his Eastern turban; Shelley, looking startled; Coleridge, broad and large as life; the Brontës on a primitive canvas painted by their brother, the canvas by which we alone know them. There is a fascinating relationship between the painter or sculptor who, with his plastic resources, gives us the visual appearance of a life and a personality, and the biographer who traces these features in an essay or book. It is fairly obvious that a painted portrait or a chiseled bust cannot be a total biography. But at its best, when the bust or the portrait comes from the hand of a master, it is certainly more than a mask, it is an essence of a life, usually a great life, and it captures—when painterly eyes and shaping hands have looked and seized it—certain individual traits and features and preserves them for posterity, for that life beyond life, of which Milton so eloquently spoke. Biography seeks to arrive at similar essences. I speak inevitably of the large figures, of endowed renderings. We need not concern ourselves with "camp" biographies or daubs, the ephemeral figures of movie stars, dope addicts, Boston stranglers; they belong to certain kinds of life histories written by journalists in our time. They belong in a wax works. They are documentary and often vividly mythic; they are more related to the photographic, the visual moment, the changing world of entertainment or crime, the great and flourishing field of interminable gossip disseminated by the media. This is quite distinct, as we know, from serious artistic biographical and pictorial quests to capture the depths and mysteries of singular greatness.

There are painted portraits then that are mere facades; there are biographies that are mere compendiums. Thomas Sergeant Perry, an early American critic, long ago described the latter. "The biographer," he wrote, "gets a dustcart into which he shovels diaries, reminiscences, old letters, until the cart is full. Then he dumps the load in front of your door. That is Vol. I. Then he goes forth again on the same errand. And there is Vol. II. Out of this rubbish the reader constructs a biography." A compendium is like a family album: a series of pictures, selections from an archive. The biographer producing such a work often pretends that he is allowing the character to speak for himself or herself. This is an ingenuous way of avoiding biographical responsibility. That responsibility involves not only accumulating and offering facts: it entails the ability to interpret these facts in the light of all that the biographer has learned about his subject. The general public, reading biographies with delight, seems unaware of how they originate. And criticism seems to me to be wholly negligent in not informing them. I know of no critics in modern times (and in an age that has given itself more to criticism than to creation) who have chosen to deal with biography as one deals with poetry or the novel. The critics fall into the easy trap of writing pieces about the life that was lived, when their business is to discuss how the life was told. Perhaps this is because biography seems to them a mix of too many things—like the opera. It involves reportage, research, interrogation of witnesses, village or urban gossip, staged events, arranged scenes, the laws of evidence, massed documents and archives, kinescopes, tape recordings, and who knows, maybe computers as well, in addition to photographs and statues with broken noses. Yet out of this material the marvelous can emerge—the story of a given life. And when such a story is read, the readers forget that it has been fashioned out of facts and words. They seem to think, like Walter Cronkite, that this is the way it is—when this is not at all the way it is: for everything is seen through particular eyes, like the painter's portrait. "How," exclaimed Virginia Woolf when she sat down to write the life of the critic and artist Roger Fry, "how can one make a life of six cardboard boxes full of tailors' bills, love letters and old picture postcards?" How indeed! This is perhaps our little secret, and it baffles the critics. The biographer, after all, is as much of a storyteller as the novelist or historian; indeed, he is a specialized kind of historian. And we have only to read Virginia Woolf's biography of Roger Fry to discover how she brilliantly shifted from the art that imagines its facts to the art that imagines the form into which facts must be put. In summary, condensation, and vivid pictorial effect I consider Mrs. Woolf's *Roger Fry* one of the most beautiful biographical portraits of our time. Here, for example, is the beginning of her chapter on the post-Impressionists:

> To a stranger meeting him then for the first time (1910) he looked much older than his age. He was only forty-four, but he gave the

impression of a man with a great weight of experience behind him. He looked worn and seasoned, ascetic yet tough. And there was his reputation, of course, to confuse a first impression—his reputation as a lecturer and as an art critic. . . . He talked that spring in a room looking out over the trees of a London square, in a deep voice like a harmonious growl. . . . Behind his glasses, beneath bushy black eyebrows, he had very luminous eyes with a curious power of observation in them as if, while he talked, he looked, and considered what he saw. Half-consciously he would stretch out a hand and begin to alter the flowers in a vase, or pick up a bit of china, turn it round and put it down again.

I have presented enough here to suggest to you how, in the hands of an artist, the word can be used to paint a portrait. In one hundred words Virginia Woolf paints a picture, ready to be hung, of Roger Fry at forty-four. In these few sentences she has told us a great deal not only about his appearance, his eyes, his physical being, but also his character, the restlessness of it, the energy of his fingers reaching out, touching the shape of things, composing, arranging.

I have often said that a biographer is a storyteller who may not invent his facts but who is allowed to imagine his form. He is like the sculptor who doesn't invent his clay, or the painter who doesn't invent the tubes out of which he squeezes his paint. The biographical imagination is exercised upon gathered data; and the squeezed colors may not be mixed or blended. They can only be arranged. Biography is the art of human portrayal in words, and it is a noble and adventurous art. There are many ways of making portraits. We know how a painter can give voices to an entire wall; and how a sculptor with skill of eye and chisel brings durable life to marble. So a biographer fashions a man or a woman out of the seemingly intractable materials of archives, diaries, documents, dreams, a glimpse, a series of memories. The biographer who respects his craft makes his figure speak in its own voice and stance. I think this is what Lytton Strachey had in mind when he said that the biographical art was "the most delicate and humane of all the branches of the art of writing." I'm not sure that it's more humane than poetry or the novel, but it touches us just as intimately, for it tries to tell a human truth, it stands for the thousands of things and people that the portrait gallery stands for. Yeats suggested that "we may come to think that nothing exists but a stream of souls, that all knowledge is biography"—and I gladly assent to this beautiful way of seeing life because all knowledge is mixed up with what goes on in human minds and in the senses that inform our body and give shape to our being.

Biography from time to time seems to have a frightening effect on creative artists. George Eliot called it "a disease of English literature." Vladimir Nabokov described it as "psycho-plagiarism." Auden repeatedly—even while reviewing biographies with delight for the *New Yorker*—called it "always superfluous" and "usually in bad taste." Unlike Yeats, unlike Henry James who called biography "one of the great observed adventures of mankind," these artists seem to be discussing certain kinds of biography that deal in the small coin of life, not the larger treasures—and they are worried about invasion of privacy. T.S. Eliot certainly was when he ordered that no biography be sanctioned by his heirs. Thackeray had done the same earlier, as did Matthew Arnold. Eliot put the matter clearly when he said "curiosity about the private life of a public man may be of three kinds: the useful, the harmless and the impertinent." And he claimed that the line "between curiosity which is legitimate and that which is merely harmless, and between that which is merely harmless and that which is vulgarly impertinent" can never be drawn precisely. I mention these opinions to show how widely apart men of genius are in their view of life portraits. We must regard what they say about biography as individual statements reflecting personal misgivings; they do not alter the fact of biography itself; they relate rather to how it is practiced. And now I can hear you ask why I call biography a young art, when we can summon Plutarch out of olden times and Boswell out of modernity. I see these men, centuries apart, as having laid certain cornerstones in the way in which Defoe laid a cornerstone for the novel by writing *Robinson Crusoe.* Plutarch shored up for us what remained of the great legends and myths of the noble Greeks and Romans. He assembled his materials—ancient lore, old wives' tales, stories of splendors and glories, miseries and defeats—traveling the length of the Mediterranean in his historical quest. We pay homage to him as an historian who sought the meanings of great lives as a form of moral philosophy. And Shakespeare paid biography his homage when he infused into Plutarch the divine poetry by which we today know his Roman plays—Caesar, Brutus, Mark Antony, and the others. Moving to the eighteenth century, we pay homage to Boswell for creating an unique work: that of staying close to his subject for a quarter of a century and writing minutes of the great man's talk that have the ring of truth. Biography rarely possesses conversation, and Boswell gave to his life of Dr. Johnson the valuable recreation of the doctor's voice and his mind within that voice. In this sense he predicted the tape recorder and oral history—but tapes are mechanical records, unfiltered through a recording mind. Boswell, like Plutarch, is a foundation stone, not a model. Modern Boswells have ended in disaster. I have dreamed of writing an essay on them—how Robert Frost's Boswell began his work in love and adulation and ended in disparagement and hate; how Faulkner's listened to his talk of liquor and horses only to be frustrated by the writer's widow and some personal hindrance that so far he has not overcome; how Thornton Wilder named a young Boswell whose enthusiasm led Wilder to hastily withdraw; not to speak of Shaw's Boswell who wrote a fat book that bears unmistakable evidence that Shaw did much of the writing.

The great problem that we must face at the start is the oppressive weight of modern archives. Gone are the days when biographies could be written out of half a dozen shoe boxes, or pieced together out of little facts like the royal grant of wine to Chaucer, or Shakespeare's second-best bed. Fancy writing a biography out of a man's check stubs. From not having enough material, biography has come into the dubious possession of great wealth and more than it can absorb and digest. The modern archive preserves everything; entire libraries have been created for each of our recent presidents. Can a biographer afford to spend his lifetime wading through such great masses of paper, Himalayas of photographs, microfilms, kinescopes, and still emerge, if not suffocated, with any sense of a face or a personality? What comes out of these archives are books too heavy and too long. Did Lytton Strachey, that master of brevity, who put Queen Victoria into 300 pages out of *her* archives, which cover almost a century, deserve almost a thousand pages for himself? Does Rex Stout, splendid detective-story writer though he is, need 600? or Gertrude Vanderbilt Whitney? Some sense of proportion is needed. I can hear you asking me, does Henry James deserve five volumes? I won't try to answer that question now but will confine myself to saying I believe this biography to be one of the shorter biographies of our time. I admire the British when they are able to tell us in 200 pages all we need to know of certain quiet lives. We do not need—as so many biographers seem to think—a record of every last date in a subject's datebook, a catalog of gourmet dinners, and chapter and verse on every glorious drunk, when these have such simple and familiar ritualistic beginnings—and archetypal endings. Nor do we need clouds of witnesses for every life—as exemplified in the lives of the two Cranes, Stephen and Hart, which occupy 800 pages of print each, even though the subjects died at thirty. To paraphrase Ruskin, it is not pleasant to have great parts of archives flung in a reader's face; and the subject ends up fenced in by walls of quotation and abysses of anecdote. Biography still has to learn the art of the portrait. It is all too often the work of journeymen, as Lytton Strachey said. Critics, poets, novelists, should write biographies. John Berryman performed a service when he wrote a life of Stephen Crane. Virginia Woolf was doing the same when she wrote her book on Roger Fry. And Norman Mailer, whatever his motivations, revealed a proper sense of biography when as a novelist he sought to capture a figure as elusive and as delicate as Marilyn Monroe. Even if we judge his work a failure, we must praise his undertaking.

I do not disparage archives. I simply groan when I see one. Those great cluttered masses of papers, those mountains of photographs in Texas of Lyndon B., and no doubt those endless tapes that will speak to posterity, like the recorded telephone calls of Treasury Secretary Henry Morgenthau. Who is to say what should be kept and what shouldn't? I remember finding a fur neckpiece in a box that contained letters of Henry James in the Library of Congress. The fur, I was told, was public property, and it was a question whether it should be quietly burned or properly sequestered. It told me merely that the lady who had received the letters got her archive mixed with her wardrobe. Yet perhaps that mangy little fur had its place. The oddest scrap of paper sometimes takes on an awesome significance after the passage of time, and I agree with T.S. Eliot that one never knows what a laundry list will reveal. No, we must allow papers to accumulate in a laissez-faire spirit, we must allow biographical subjects to fill entire barns with their Internal Revenue records and political figures to gather the memorabilia so gratifying to their egos. Our concern is how to deal with this clutter, how to confront our subject, how to achieve the clean mastery of the portrait painter unconcerned with archives, who reads only the lines in the face, the settled mouth, the color of the cheeks, the brush strokes and pencil marks of time. More often than not this offers us the revealing mask of life. The biographer must learn to know the mask—and in doing this he will have won half the battle. The other half is his real battle, the most difficult part of his task— his search for what I call the figure under the carpet, the evidence in the reverse of the tapestry, the life-myth of a given mask. In an archive, we wade simply and securely through paper and photocopies and related concrete materials. But in our quest for the life-myth we tread on dangerous speculative and inferential ground, ground that requires all of our attention, all of our accumulated resources. For we must read certain psychological signs that enable us to understand what people are really saying behind the faces they put on, behind the utterances they allow themselves to make before the world. The aggressive emotion that masquerades as a cutting witticism; the excessive endearment that conceals a certain animus; the pleasant joking remark that is accompanied by a hostile gesture; the hostile gesture that turns into a pat on the back; the sudden slip of the tongue that says the opposite of what has been intended. This is the "psychological evidence" a biographer must learn to read, even as he learns to read the handwriting of his personality and his slips of the pen. Armed with this kind of eyesight, a biographer reads much more in the materials than any sketchers of facades. To my vision, Pope John Paul I expressed a great deal when he refused to be crowned and asked for a simplification of a ceremony old in history. By that one gesture, he told the world the course of his apostolate, brief though it was. There was a message in that decision—a message about power—which the observant might have read. And if I were writing the Pope's biography, I would start by seeking an answer to this important question.

The method I am proposing for biography is related to the methods of Sherlock Holmes and also to those of Sigmund Freud. If one approaches an archive with the right questions, one carries a series of important keys to locked doors. The right doors will open if the right questions are asked; the mountains of trivia will melt away, and essences will emerge. Many historians have unconsciously worked in this way, but I am not aware that we have consciously sought to describe a *method*. This is not easy, nor can this method be mechanically learned. It requires a certain kind of talent, a certain kind of inwardness to look at the reverse of a tapestry, to know when and where to seek the figure under the carpet.

What do I mean by the hidden personal myth? Let me take a writer like Ernest Hemingway, whose life and habits have been widely recorded, not least by a circle of his relatives and friends. We know he liked to shoot, to fish, to drink; we know that he was boastful. He wanted to be champion. He wanted to fight wars—on his own terms—and shoot big game and catch the biggest fish and live the manliest life—the super-manly life. Was not one of his books entitled *Men Without Women*? That tells us something—though it may not be what you think. Small wonder that Max Eastman asked a very proper biographical question—why did Hemingway make such a fuss about the hair on his chest? And we remember that when Hemingway ran into Eastman in Maxwell Perkins's office at Scribner's, he proved Eastman's insight by demanding a fight. The two writers ended on the floor with a great flailing of arms and legs. "I wasn't going to box with him," Eastman said when he described the incident to me. "I just put my arms around him and embraced him." Hemingway wanted to prove he had hair on his chest. Now the obvious myth—and I choose Hemingway because he can be read so easily—was the novelist's drive to do the biggest, kill the biggest, achieve the greatest, and that is written large in all his books. A code of drive and courage, simple, direct, masculine, excessively masculine; and a code in the art of trying to shape and simplify and crystallize and not get too close to feeling. That is the manifest myth. But as a biographer, I go beyond this and ask—what does Hemingway express? What is Hemingway saying to us in all his books and all his actions? A great deal, and as is nearly always the case, much that is exactly the opposite of what he seems to be saying. A manly man doesn't need to prove his masculinity every moment of the day. Only someone who is troubled and not at all secure with himself and with his role puts up his fists and spoils for a fight over a casual remark by an easygoing and affectionate person like Max Eastman. The biographical questions multiply, and in effect we ask ourselves: What is Hemingway defending himself against, so compulsive is his drive toward action and away from examined feeling, so consistent is his quest to surpass himself, as if he always must prove—even after he has had the world's acclaim—that he is the best and the greatest. Critics have remarked on this, and I say nothing that has not already been widely discussed—but it illustrates what I mean by the figure under the carpet. Hemingway's figure *in* the carpet is his pattern of seeking out violence wherever he can find it, seeking out courage, resignation, heroism, and perseverance, and avoiding too much feeling. But the reverse of the tapestry tells us that somewhere within resides a troubled, uncertain, insecure figure, who works terribly hard to give himself eternal assurance. Where there seems to be immense fulfillment, we discern extraordinary inadequacy—and self-flagellation and a high competitiveness; also, a singular want of generosity toward his fellow artists, since he must always proclaim himself the champ. Life reduced to the terms of the bullring and the prize fight is a very narrow kind of life indeed. The biography of Hemingway that captures the real portrait, the portrait within, still needs to be written. And what is important in Hemingway's archive, which is large, are the answers to the questions that will relate his doubts, his failures, his struggles, and not the answers to his successes that are written in the public prints.

I will now take an example less obvious and less well-known—that of Henry David Thoreau. The biographers of Thoreau have always accepted his view of himself and his mission at Walden Pond "to suck the marrow of life," that is, to meditate and learn the virtues of simplicity and solitude, and not be a slave to the bondages of life, like mortgages and banks and the humdrum entanglements of the farmer for whom Thoreau expresses considerable contempt. *Walden* is a beautiful book, an exquisite distillation of the intentions and desires of Thoreau, a work of the imagination that pretends it is a true story, and it embodies a myth that all America—indeed the whole world—has adopted: that of getting away from the slavery of civilization, facing the world as God made it, not as man ravaged it. This is one part of Thoreau's story, and it is a part of his greatness. The question a biographer seeking the truth must equally ask if he wants to see the figure under Thoreau's carpet is, what motivated him to this idealistic undertaking? Why did he decide to built a hut? In other words, why beyond his own beautiful rationalizations—did he *really* go to Walden pond? That seems to be a difficult question to answer. Yet by focusing on it within the materials of Thoreau's life a number of answers emerge. There is that day the remarkable woodsman went fishing and in cooking the fish set fire to the woods and almost burned Concord down. There is the simple fact that the farmers had quite as much contempt for Thoreau as he had for them. There is the evidence that Concord thought him a man of enormous talent who idled his time away walking in the woods. There is the man who said he'd rather shake the outstretched branch of a tree than the hand of Henry Thoreau. And there is Emerson who quoted this over Thoreau's grave. Thoreau's hut, we learn, did not stand in great loneliness; he did not plant it in a wilderness. He planted it on Emerson's land on the shores of Walden with Emerson's consent. This made it easy for him to criticize those who had to pay rent or mortgages. The railway lay within easy distance. His mother's house was one mile down the road and, said the Boston hostess, Annie Fields, in her diary, David Thoreau was a *very* good son, "even when living in his retirement at Walden Pond, he would come home every day." Others have told us that he raided the family cookie jar while describing how he subsisted on the beans he grew in his field. To discover this, and to remember how often Thoreau dined with the Emersons, and gregariously joined the citizens of Concord around the cracker barrel in the local store, is to overlook his life struggle, the inner biographical problem that the literary portrait painter must face. The evidence can be read in the moving parable within the pages of *Walden*, which tells us more than a thousand letters might in an archive. Thoreau wrote: "I long ago lost a hound, a bay horse, and a turtle dove, and am still on their trail. Many are the travellers I have spoken concerning them, describing their tracks and what calls they answer to. I have met one or two who had heard the hound, and the tramp of the horse, and even seen the dove disappear behind a cloud, and they seemed as anxious to recover them as if they had lost them themselves."

Loss and anxiety about loss—a bay horse, a hound, a turtle dove. Thoreau's little parable, which he launches enigmatically in *Walden*, contains a great deal that a biographer needs to guide him into the reverse of the tapestry of the author of *Walden*. Here, in capsule, are the three members of the animal kingdom closest to mankind: the faithful hound, guide, protector, loving and lovable; the horse of Thoreau's time, plower of fields, the embodiment of strength, trust, and support, and the spirited symbol of all that is instinctual in man; and finally the turtle dove, the soft cooing swift messenger, bearer of tidings as in the Bible, symbol of love and of the Holy Ghost. The biographer of Thoreau must write not the story of a solitude-loving, nature-loving, eternally questing self-satisfied isolator who despises his neighbors, and is despised by them, but the story of a man who feels he has lost the deepest parts of himself—without guide and support, without strength and love, a lost little boy of Concord, a loner, a New England narcissus. The biography would have to be written not in a debunking spirit but in compassion and with the realization that this man who felt he had lost so much was able to transcend his losses and create an American myth and the work of art known as *Walden*.

Biography stated in these terms begins to become more than a recital of facts, more than a description of an individual's minute doings, more than a study of achievement, when we allow ourselves to glimpse the myths within and behind the individual, the inner myth we all create in order to live, the myth that tells us we have some being, some selfhood, some goal, something to strive for beyond the fulfillments of food or sex or creature comforts. I remember a young man who set out to write the life of Rex Stout, the creator of Nero Wolfe. He asked me how to go about his job. I found rising within me, out of unconscious dictation, the sentence: "You will have to find out why Rex, a king, sought to disguise himself as Nero, an emperor—and a bad emperor at that!" Those of us who still remember Rex Stout might have thought he had kingly ambitions, for he founded Freedom House, he fought for copyright, he became head of countless enlightened organizations. And he wrote a series of books in which a very benign fat man with an evil name, living in isolation, solves crimes and punishes miscreants and makes the good prevail. Indeed he hires a legman whose name is Goodwin—a winner of good. Do not laugh when I play with the nomenclature of biographical subjects: the names by which we are called, the names we call ourselves, these too are part of our myth. Rex Stout was a thin man and he made Nero Wolfe very stout indeed, 260 pounds, thus reversing the saying that in every stout man a thin man struggles to be freed. But if he had imperial dreams, why such a bad emperor? One can discover easily where the Wolfe comes from. Rex Stout's middle name was Todhunter—which is Scots for a fox hunter. So we see the series of metamorphoses, king-emperor, fox-wolf, thin-stout. An earlier detective created by Stout was named Tecumseh Fox—and this demonstrates how consistent the imagination of myth can be: Tecumseh was a very imperial Shawnee. Such literary games are amusing enough; they become more fascinating, however, when examined in the light of psychology. We learn in our inquiries that Rex Stout, in creating opposites of himself, was also consciously creating opposites of Sherlock Holmes, who was, as it happened, a tall thin man like Stout himself. He once told an inquirer he had decided that Arthur Conan Doyle was the king of detective-story writers (how inescapable the designation "king") and, since he wanted the same kind of kingship, he decided to make Nero Wolfe the opposite in every way to Sherlock Holmes. Holmes played the violin, Wolfe raised orchids; Holmes took cocaine, Wolfe drank beer; Holmes went anywhere to solve a crime, Wolfe stayed at home.

This tells us that Rex Stout was engaged in a double process—that of creating a persona involving himself and an opposite to Doyle's detective with whom he was identified. He did something else. He followed Doyle in creating an American Dr. Watson who is Watson's opposite too—Archie Goodwin is as bright and keen as Watson is genially dull and phlegmatic. If we go back to look at Stout and Doyle themselves we discover that both were living out in their imaginations a king-myth or an emperor-myth. What fun it was for Doyle, a hard-working Victorian doctor turned author, to cut loose in his imagination and become Sherlock Holmes, to visit in fancy iniquitous dens, take drugs, and play a moody fiddle, while also retaining the bluff phlegmatic Victorian, Dr. Watson. What is this duality of the common self and the fantasy self but the creative and imaginative man tied to the usual and the routine and the bondage of society, seeking to escape by putting his literal and prosaic self into a persona—Dr. Watson or Archie Goodwin? On the other hand the imaginative self achieves freedoms beyond common reach, including victories over Scotland Yard or Manhattan police inspectors. I suspect that Doyle got most of his fun in life out of being Sherlock Holmes. But I discern, without going deeply into the matter, more trouble than fun for Rex Stout, who somehow had to choose the name of evil, that of a bad emperor rather than a good one, who turned foxes into wolves, because he perhaps was a bit afraid of his imperial dreams, and had some guilt about them. That need not concern us here. Let us leave the solution to future biographers. I think I have sufficiently shown the way in which we often play games of secret sharer—Joseph Conrad's term—with our mythic selves. The creative artist ends by turning his fantasies and problems into works that bring the fame and power that is sought—even as political figures through their acts create their public personae, even as our generals on occasion become their myths on the battlefield. In writing the lives of such men we find ourselves involved in a truly great adventure, and not merely that of archeological digging among their archives, which any well-instructed graduate student can do. We go beyond this necessary routine into the search for an individual's hidden dreams of himself, and then discover how they have been acted out, either in an elaborate and imaginative defense against guilts and anxieties, as in Hemingway or Thoreau, or in a series of fantasy conversions or metamorphoses, as in Stout and Doyle. The biographer who writes the life of his subject's self-concept passes through a facade into the inner house of life.

We must recognize and not resist the modern explorations of the unconscious, the marvelous id-being with which we are endowed and where so many mysterious parts of life are enacted. This has opened up great new provinces for biographical knowledge and biographical exploration. What I enunciate is, I believe, a new principle for biography that has only just been adumbrated—that the writings and utterances and acts of any subject contain many more secrets of character and personality than we have hitherto allowed. A secret myth, as well as a manifest myth, as I say, is hidden within every creative life, and, in the gestures of a politician, the strategies of a general, the canvases and statues of art and the life-styles of charismatic characters, we may discover more than biography has ever discovered in the past. Whole case histories can be compiled out of revealed experience—but we must compile them in the language of literature, not the language of therapy. We understand much more now about behavior and motivation. We understand much more how the rational mind, in concert with our senses, indulges in fantasies and sometimes translates these into realities. There are so many new ways, then, for drawing larger conclusions about an inner life, of which the outer life is a constant expression. Some such principles come to us from the new psychology.

The National Portrait Gallery in London recently held a fascinating exhibition. They carefully gathered a series of portraits painted by the moderns—those who no longer paint faces simply as they see them. It was an exhibition that showed how cubists, vorticists, impressionists, and the other innovators of our time sought to put on canvas living subjects created out of new visions of reality. I would have difficulty describing in words the many rich things these portrait painters did—but it will best illustrate my point if I say to you that in Roland Penrose's portrait of his wife, he depicted in his surrealism birds and butterflies clustering along the mouth and eyes. And we know how revolutionary is Picasso's portrait of Gertrude Stein. I cannot remember when I found an exhibition more exhilarating. For what I saw was that these modern painters and sculptors—Picasso and Giacometti, Kokoschka and Matisse, Modigliani and Tchelitchev, and the earlier Gaudier-Brzeska—had all done exactly what I am saying the biographer must now do: they sought to go behind the facade, to penetrate the mask. There was Wyndham Lewis's Edith Sitwell, in which that lady was reduced to her flat-voiced impassivity, or Sickert's portrait of Edward VIII that caught in a strange and remarkable way that poor monarch's low self-esteem. Giacometti said of his sculptured portraits, "The adventure, the great adventure, is to see something unknown appear each day in the same face," and Picasso, speaking of his Gertrude Stein, said, "Everybody thinks she is not at all like her portrait but never mind, in the end she will manage to look just like it." Notable in the exhibition was Dali's portrait of Isabel Styles in which he managed to convey both external aspect and inner fantasy.

It was Graham Sutherland who best stated the case for biography in this exhibition. "I think it is true," he said, "that only those totally without physical vanity, educated in painting, or with exceptionally good manners, can disguise their feelings of shock or even revulsion when they are confronted for the first time with a reasonable truthful image of themselves."

For me these modern painters had with consistency carried the truths of their art into their representation of living persons as they had of landscape and rooms and the things that surround us in our world. They sought the inwardness and the myth; they did what Van Gogh did when he painted a chair or a picture of himself. They moved from the splendid verisimilitude of Rembrandt's self-portraits to a kind of Ur-portrait. In the recreation of lives, we have reached a time when we must, like these painters, give a new account of ourselves. We must not flinch from the realities we have discovered; we must realize that beyond the flesh and the legend there is an inner sense of self, an inner man or woman, who shapes and expresses, alters and clothes, the personality that is our subject and our art. Archives become then simply illustrative—and by the method of seeking the secret self, the inner myth, our subjects stand revealed—not in the papers they accumulated but the works they wrought, the acts they performed, the shape they gave to their existence.

JUSTIN KAPLAN
The Naked Self
and Other Problems

A part from the name given him at birth, "there's really very little that a man can change at will," Saul Bellow wrote in *Seize the Day*. By taking a new name, as his protagonist, Tommy Wilhelm did, an unfinished person may hope to enter into more dynamic—but not necessarily more intimate—transactions, both with the world outside and with his or her "true soul," the naked self. The twenty-five-year-old Ernesto Guevara, called "El Chancho," the Slob, became "El Che," or Buddy. "The most important and cherished part of my life," he said a few years before he was captured and executed in Bolivia, was the new name, "Che." "Everything that came before it, my surname and my Christian name, are minor, personal, and insignificant details." Lenin, Trotsky, Stalin, Malcolm X: such names, all assumed, not given, also suggest that the change is more than nominal—it is organic, revolutionary.

For reasons of psychic as well as aural euphony, David Henry Thoreau altered the order of his names and became Henry David Thoreau. Nathaniel Hawthorne revised the spelling of his family name, adding the "w." The death of Henry James, Senior, liberated his novelist son from the demeaning "appendage" of *"mere* junior"—he had disliked it for forty years, "with my dislike never in the least understood or my state pitied." (The word "junior," Leon Edel says, "had a diminishing sound.") Willa Cather found her way from the baptismal "Wilella" through "Willa Love Cather," "Willa Lova Cather," and a fantasy identity, "William Cather, M.D.," to the name she signed her will with, "Willa Sibert Cather." She took the "Sibert" from an uncle on her mother's side who was killed fighting for the Confederacy and became his "namesake," she wrote in 1902, three years before she published her first book of short stories and ten years before her first novel. The evolution of her name was an intimate part of her evolving vocation. At the other end of the critical scale, a young man named Pearl Grey of Zanesville, Ohio, was resigned to following in the footsteps of his father, a "tooth-puller," until he took a trip to Arizona and soon after started becoming rich and famous as Zane Grey, author of *Riders of the Purple Sage* and other horse operas. Nathan Weinstein, born in New York City in 1903, went through a Schilleresque phase as Nathaniel von Wallenstein Weinstein before arriving in Paris in 1927 as the novelist Nathanael West. The new name expressed "the new identity he had invented," says West's biographer, Jay Martin—he had become "a new man by an act of his own will."

One could cite many other writers—George Sand, George Eliot, and George Orwell, in one affinity group—who made names for themselves in this way. One could cite the preeminent authority on identity development, Erik Erikson, who in so naming himself becomes his own father. As the writer Ted Morgan—formerly Sanche de Gramont— suggests in *On Becoming American,* there may be an entire book to be written about the significance and dynamics of name changes. But for the moment two instances deserve attention. They are the most dramatic in American letters.

In 1863, when he was twenty-seven, a western journalist writing a travel letter to his paper from Carson City in the

Nevada Territory, described himself as feeling "very much as if I had just awakened from a long sleep." He signed the piece, "Yours, dreamily, Mark Twain." This first known appearance in print of the pseudonym corresponded to a discovery Samuel Clemens announced to his brother shortly after. "I have had a 'call' to literature, of a low order—*i.e.*, humorous. It is nothing to be proud of, but it is my strongest suit." He had decided to turn his talents "to seriously scribbling to excite the *laughter* of God's creatures. Poor, pitiful business!" Much later in his career, when he was well on his way to international celebrity, Clemens offered an official or canonical "history of the *nom de plume* I bear": he said he took "Mark Twain"—the leadsman's call meaning two fathoms, or twelve feet, of depth—from a Mississippi pilot, Captain Isaiah Sellers, "who used to write river news over it for the *New Orleans Picayune*. He died in 1863 and as he could no longer need that signature, I laid violent hands upon it without asking the permission of the proprietor's remains." But this history doesn't wash any better than some of the others— including a dubious saloon story about marking up two drinks on credit—that have been advanced by Clemens himself, his biographers, and assorted folklorists and hagiographers. In minor respects, too, the name is confusing to this day. Is it "Mark" or "Twain" for short, or should you—properly, I think—use the indivisible nom de plume entire?

Despite all the obfuscation several things are reasonably clear. In all likelihood Samuel Clemens simply invented the name "Mark Twain." It comes from the river, a timeless symbol of the creative unconscious; he invested it with a "magical" or "occult" significance; and, looking down the vistas of predestination that stretched all the way back to Adam's first disobedience, he said that the name with which he signed his Carson City letter "was the cause of my presently dropping out of journalism and into literature." The new name put a liberating distance between the writer-humorist-performer-celebrity and the stubbornly private

Samuel L. Clemens, although it is not so easy as it may at first seem to say which of these, Mr. Clemens or Mark Twain, is the name his naked self answers to. It is the edgy traffic between these identities, and others, that engages our interest.

One final instance of a new name both shaping and reflecting a new identity: A few weeks before his thirty-sixth birthday, Walter Whitman, former printer, schoolteacher, housebuilder, and newspaper editor, now the author, proprietor, and publisher of a literary work in press, registered a copyright with the clerk of the United States District Court for the Southern District of New York. When it went on sale in July, his book was as arresting in format and detail as in its contents: the most brilliant and original poetry yet written on the continent, at once the fulfillment of American literary romanticism and the beginnings of American literary modernism. The reader's eye was caught first by the unidentified frontispiece portrait of a bearded man dressed like a common seaman or laborer. The title page offered no clues to the author's identity. It displayed only the words "Leaves of Grass," a small decorative rule, and the legend, "Brooklyn, New York: 1855." The copyright page was more informative, but the Walter Whitman named in the statutory boilerplate was conceivably the author's publisher or assignee or even, as some readers might have concluded, a conservator appointed in cases of mental instability. Ten pages of prose eccentrically punctuated with strings of periods were followed by eighty-three pages of verse, at first glance clusters of prose sentences printed like Bible verses; the twelve poems were untitled except for the insistent head caption for each, "Leaves of Grass." Only in a passage on page 29 did the reader finally come upon a connection between the bearded loafer of the frontispiece, the anonymous author, and the copyright holder:

> Walt Whitman, an American, one of the roughs, a kosmos,
> Disorderly, fleshy and sensual . . . . eating drinking and breeding,

> No sentimentalist . . . no stander above men or women or
> apart from them . . . . no more modest than immodest.

In an era of triple-barreled literary eminences who uttered their names in Jovian trochees and dactyls—William Cullen Bryant, John Greenleaf Whittier, Ralph Waldo Emerson, Henry Wadsworth Longfellow, James Russell Lowell—the poet of *Leaves of Grass* chose to follow the populist examples of Andy Jackson, Kit Carson, and Davy Crockett. (Along with "Walter," for purposes of public discussion he rejected the cooly formal "Whitman." "I like best to have the *full name* always," he was to say. The official name "Walt Whitman" was meant to be, but never became, as indivisible as "Mark Twain." "Give both words," he said, "and don't be afraid of the tautology.") It seems that he had found his true name:

> What am I after all but a child, pleas'd with the sound of
>   my own name? repeating it over and over;
> I stand apart to hear—it never tires me.

The name "Mark Twain" established a distance. The name "Walt Whitman" put its bearer on a more familiar footing, which he frequently expressed in sexual imagery, with his "soul." He knew this entity to be "distinct from his ordinary conscious personality," as F.O. Matthiessen noted, but on the other hand it is not altogether what we would call "the unconscious." It has a dimension of transcendency. "I cannot understand the mystery," Whitman said in an early prose fragment, "but I am always conscious of myself as two—as my soul and I: and I reckon it is the same with all men and women." He teases the mystery of what he calls "the Me myself," and he mocks biography:

> And is this then (said I) what the author calls a man's life?
> And so will some one when I am dead and gone write my life?
> (As if any man really knew aught of my life,
> Why even I myself I often think know little or nothing of my real life,
> Only a few hints, a few diffused faint clews and indirections. . . .

But on at least one occasion in his life before he wrote

Leaves of Grass, the "I" experienced such a heightened and ecstatic sense of communion with the "soul" that all reality, subjective and objective, the Me and the Not-Me, became seamless:

> I believe in you my soul, the other I am must not abase
>   itself to you,
> And you must not be abased to the other,

he wrote in a celebrated passage that called up for himself and his reader "a transparent summer morning" of illumination:

> Swiftly arouse and spread around me the peace and knowledge
>   that pass all the argument of the earth,
> And I know that the hand of God is the promise of my own,
> And I know that the Spirit of God is the brother of my own,
> And that all the men ever born are also my brothers, and the
>   women my sisters and lovers,
> And that a kelson of the creation is love . . .

Just as Samuel Clemens awoke from "a long sleep" to sign himself "Mark Twain," Whitman awoke from the first half of his life and was dazzled by the "happiness" he saw:

> I cannot be awake, for nothing looks to me as it did before,
> Or else I am awake for the first time, and all before has
>   been a mean sleep.

"Whether it was 'cosmic' or mundane," the critic David Cavitch writes in a recent essay called "Whitman's Mystery," "some kind of illumination uplifted [him] from the mediocrity of his early writings and pulled down the walls of his shallow, adolescent egocentricity. He became, instead, profoundly egocentric." Whitman's egocentricity, it might be added, was not only profound but also so sweeping that he projects himself over the roofs of the universe and into every corner of existence. As Tolstoy remarked about Lincoln, he "wanted to see himself in the world—not the world in himself." The "I" speaking in Whitman's poems ceases to be specific and personal and becomes generic, archetypal. If *Leaves of Grass* had to have a subtitle, it might well be Gertrude Stein's *Everybody's Autobiography.*

For a number of reasons it seems altogether fitting, in an essay sponsored by the National Portrait Gallery, to go on dealing with Whitman, who probably sat to more portraitists, sculptors, and photographers than any American writer of his time. And the building in which the National Portrait Gallery is housed, originally the United States Patent Office, is as intimately associated with Whitman as his birthplace or the raddled old shanty he died in at Camden, New Jersey.

Still unfinished when he first came to it during the wartime winter of 1862-63, the Patent Office impressed him as the "noblest of Washington buildings," a Greek revival shrine of American ingenuity. Its great halls were normally the repository of models representing, as he said, "every kind of utensil, machine or invention, it ever enter'd into the mind of man to conceive." But in the aftermath of Bull Run, Shiloh, Antietam, and Fredericksburg, overflow casualties from the military hospitals were packed into the Patent Office, with rows of sick, wounded, and dying soldiers lying in the aisles between glass display cases. "There was a gallery running above the hall in which there were beds also," Whitman wrote in February 1863. "It was, indeed, a curious scene, especially at night when lit up. The glass cases, the beds, the forms lying there, the gallery above, and the marble pavement under foot—the suffering, and the fortitude to bear it in various degrees—occasionally, from some, the groan that could not be repress'd—sometimes a poor fellow dying, with emaciated face and glassy eye, the nurse by his side, the doctor also there, but no friend, no relative—such were the sights but lately in the Patent-office." It was in such places of suffering that Whitman found his wartime occupation: "wound-dresser."

> Aroused and angry,
> I thought to beat the alarum, and urge relentless war;
> But soon my fingers fail'd me, my face droop'd, and I
>   resign'd myself.
> To sit by the wounded and soothe them, or silently watch
>   the dead.

Two years later, when the tide of war had turned for good in this makeshift city, the same halls and galleries were the scene of Abraham Lincoln's Second Inaugural Ball. "I have been up to look at the dance and supper-rooms," Whitman wrote, "and I could not help thinking, what a different scene they presented to my view a while since, fill'd with a crowded mass of the worst wounded of the war . . . To-night, beautiful women, perfumes, the violin's sweetness, the polka and the waltz; then the amputation, the blue face, the groan, the glassy eye of the dying, the clotted rag, the odor of wounds and blood." By this time he had finally managed to land a clerkship with the Interior Department and was assigned to the Indian Bureau, located in the Patent Office basement. The job was "easy enough," he told his brother. "I take things very easy—the rule is to come at 9 and go at 4— but I don't come at 9, and only stay till 4 when I want." At his government desk and on government time he was busily preparing a new edition of *Leaves of Grass.* His blue paperbound copy of an earlier edition, with his notes in ink and three colors of pencil and his folded, fragile inserts and interleavings, is one of the chief artifacts in Whitman archeology and brings us directly into the presence of the poet at work.

In the course of a "loyalty," "fidelity," and "moral character" check on employees of the Interior Department, this personal copy was removed from Whitman's desk and brought to the secretary, James Harlan. He found its contents, in particular its messages of sexual liberation, "outrageous," but it is possible that his reasons for firing Whitman abruptly also had to do with a prudent administrator's intolerance for sinecures and deadwood. Nevertheless, Whitman's disciples, skilled and dedicated polemicists, ignored the fact that a hundred and more employees had also been purged at the same time and compared Whitman's pink slip to the hemlock given Socrates and the vinegar and gall given Jesus. According to H.L. Mencken, this familiar episode deserves to be commemorated yearly in "our accustomed houses of worship"—it had brought together "the greatest poet America has ever produced" with "the damndest ass." In the hands of the disciples, Whitman's dismissal crystallized a messianic pattern of gospel, persecution, and passion, and generated a new avatar: "The Good Gray Poet," Christ-figure, guru. But here biography begins to turn into the history of a reputation and perhaps loses sight of the inner life, the growth of the naked self from its earliest shivering state.

Self-made man and self-made poet, Whitman nevertheless took considerable pride in his ancestors: English and Dutch settlers who came over in the seventeenth century prospered as landowners and farmers on Long Island, and fought with valor in the Revolution. In the burial ground near Huntington he could see his "whole family history . . . three centuries concentrate[d] on this sterile acre." Yet, to use one of Whitman's constitutive metaphors, this sterile acre was also a compost heap drawing sweet life out of the sour dead. Both Whitman and the grass he celebrated were "tomb blossoms," the title of one of his first pieces of prose fiction. "I guess the grass is itself a child," he wrote in "Song of Myself,"

And now it seems to me the beautiful uncut hair of graves.

As he grew toward a consciousness of the ancestral and historical past, the young Whitman was confronted with patterns of decline. A generation of revolutionary heroes, warriors, and signers of the Declaration of Independence was dying off day by day. It seemed that the time of his growing up was a long farewell to a receding world of purpose and rectitude. As the young nation fed on dreams of untold natural wealth and manifest destiny, Whitman's family was sinking in the social and economic order. The Long Island farms and houses passed into other hands; centuries of rootedness gave way to a rhythm of subdivision, foreclosure, and dispossession that accelerated as he grew up and perhaps suggested to him that change and loss went hand in hand. Between 1823 and 1835—that is, between Whitman's fourth and sixteenth years—his parents moved approximately twelve times.

Change and loss also had a genetic counterpart. Of the eight Whitman children who survived infancy one was a genius, three were normal, and four were disasters. The oldest was difficult from the start, grew moody and dangerously violent, and was finally committed by Walt to a lunatic asylum, where he died. The youngest was born feebleminded and maimed and also had to be institutionalized. In between were a sister, who was clearly psychotic, and a brother, who was an alcoholic and whose wife, also an alcoholic, became a prostitute after he died. From such a background came Walt Whitman, chief American celebrant of what William James called "the religion of healthy-mindedness." How he did this—whether in reaction, compensation, self-protection, whether willfully or inexplicably—is one of the mysteries the biographer must at least describe if not hope to "solve."

The inner life of a creative person "is as much a work of fiction—of guiding narrative structures—as novels and poems," Phyllis Rose says in her study of Virginia Woolf, *Woman of Letters;* "the task of literary biography is to explore this fiction," this "personal mythology." This may be what Yeats had in mind when he said, "There is some one Myth for every man, which, if we but knew it, would make us understand all that he did and thought." Often the biographer has to suspend historical hindsight in order to deal imaginatively and empathetically with what Sir Thomas Browne called *Pseudodoxia Epidemica,* or *Vulgar Errors,* bits, pieces, and even entire structures of belief that now appear downright silly but at one time served a purpose: they supplied the underpinnings of personal mythologies. For the biographer, who is concerned with rendering another person's texture and density of experience in another era, the supporting belief is of immense interest, whatever its present validity and even though it may fall in a class with Browne's snails that have no eyes and elephants that have no joints and, unlike other "pedestrious Animals," sleep standing up, leaning against trees.

Whitman offers us a demonstration of how it is possible to reach the right conclusions by reasoning from the wrong data. As he entered the decade of his thirties, a familiar time for radical redefinitions of the self, he became a sort of storage battery or accumulator for ephemeral orthodoxies, among them phrenology, animal magnetism, and "hydropathy," or water cure. The latter dispensation was supposedly discovered by a peasant, Vincent Priessnitz, when he immersed his aching bones in the rills and streams of Austrian Silesia. During the 1840s, hydropathy became big business in New York, already a world market center for all sorts of schemes promising social and individual happiness. James Russell Lowell, President Eliphalet Nott of Union College, James Fenimore Cooper, Professor Calvin E. Stowe of Cincinnati, and his wife Harriet Beecher Stowe were among the sufferers who came from far and near to have their body poisons flushed away by enemas, wet packs, long soaks, cascades, and other means of "exomosis" or "trans-udation" employing pure Croton water. Whatever its long-range effectiveness, the water cure was bracing to the spirits and a sovereign treatment for alcoholism, hangovers, and colonic stasis. Some of its practices leaked into general acceptance and encouraged water drinking, frequent baths, and simple diets. This was no small gain in a time of intemperance, low standards of personal cleanliness, and huge meals of greasy batter-plated meats and underbaked breads stoked away when their already dyspeptic victims were at the gallop or comatose with exhaustion and surfeit.

Meanwhile, America had welcomed as a messiah Johann Kaspar Spurzheim, one of the founders of phrenology, as he had named it—the science of the mind. He was teaching a course in brain anatomy at the Harvard Medical School when he died. His sudden departure was memorialized by the Massachusetts Medical Association as "a calamity to mankind." His body went to Mount Auburn Cemetery, and his brain went to Harvard, but his happy spirit marched the length and breadth of the continent for more than thirty years.

According to Spurzheim, the faculties of the mind had specific localities in the folds and fissures of the brain. The size of these localities varied according to the strength or weakness of individual faculties in individual brains, but since the skull, as described, was a bony fabric that fitted the brain like the skin of a pumpkin, it was possible to measure individual faculties from the outside. The examination and classification of living skulls—"bump reading"—was a form of palpation, the classic diagnostic procedure applied this time not to livers, uteruses, and prostates but to personality, temperament, and ability. The corollary of Spurzheim's elegant propositions was electrifying: If you found out what you were, you could then become what you wanted to be by "depressing" faculties that were too prominent and "elevating" those that were too small. It seemed that the race had found a way of purging itself of crime, insanity, and bafflement and was about to grow upward toward perfection. For Americans in particular, already fired with self-reliance and democratic mission, Spurzheim's teachings were like drinks on the house.

"One of the choice places of New York to me then," Whitman said of the five or six years before the emergence of *Leaves of Grass*, "was the 'Phrenological Cabinet' of Fowler & Wells, Nassau street near Beekman. . . . I went there often, and once for myself had a very elaborate and leisurely examination and 'chart of bumps.' I have it yet," he added; he should also have added that on three separate occasions he published it as a pedigree or charter for his poetry. In addition to phrenological readings, Fowler & Wells conducted a

"Hydropathic and Physiological School," dispensed information about roughage, diet, high colonics, and the like, published a number of mass-circulation periodicals in the field, and also espoused the cause of animal magnetism, yet another European import. The universe was represented as a vast battery of "irradiating power" or "nervous force" that worked on electrical principles conveniently confused with those of the magnetic telegraph. Men and women, horses, cows, and chickens, maples, cornstalks, and raspberry canes, rocks and ponds were all part of a network of sending and receiving stations that relayed an invisible electric fluid from the strong to the weak by means of proximity, contact, hypnosis, arcane passes, handholding, and more intimate techniques of stimulation. Like phrenology, animal magnetism bridged mind and matter, the individual and the mass, and was supposed to cure disease and extend life.

In time, the poet of *Leaves of Grass* sang "the body electric" and announced,

> Mine is no callous shell,
> I have instant conductors all over me whether I pass or stop,
> They seize every object and lead it harmlessly through me.

The sexual force itself was magnetic:

> Does the earth gravitate? does not all matter, aching,
>   attract all other matter?
> So the body of me to all I meet or know.

Hypnotist and clairvoyant,

> Bending with open eyes over the shut eyes of sleepers,

the poet saw mankind bound together by mesmeric flow and electric touch:

> The sleepers are very beautiful as they lie unclothed.
> They flow hand in hand over the whole earth from east to
>   west as they lie unclothed.

"Well-begotten and rais'd by a perfect mother," the poet also

boasted beautiful blood and a beautiful brain, perfect health
from top to toe:

> I do not press my fingers across my mouth,
> I keep as delicate around the bowels as around the head
> and heart . . . .

> Divine am I inside and out, and I make holy whatever I
> touch or am touch'd from,
> The scent of these arm-pits aroma finer than prayer.

"This man has a grand physical constitution, and power
to live to a good old age," according to the Fowler & Wells
reading of Whitman's bumps. "He is undoubtedly descended
from the soundest and hardiest stock . . . Leading traits of
character appear to be Friendship, Sympathy, Sublimity and
Self-Esteem, and markedly among his combinations the
dangerous faults of Indolence, a tendency to the pleasure of
Voluptuousness and Alimentativeness, and a certain reckless
swing of animal will." Reassured by phrenology, Whitman
was to be a perfected man and also a new type of poet: robust,
sensual, joyous, a universal sharer, lover, companion, and
teacher. Poe's Roderick Usher, presiding over the fall of his
doomed house, represented in all its self-destructiveness and
brief brilliance the "Nervous Temperament" that phrenologists associated with poets and artists. Usher was cadaver-
ous in complexion, like Poe himself. His skin had "a ghostly
pallor"; his hair was "silken," "of a more than web-like soft-
ness and tenuity"; his eyes were "large, liquid, and luminous
beyond comparison"; and his expression was remote from
"any idea of simple humanity."

The thirty-year-old editor who had his bumps read on
Nassau Street was soon to describe himself, in antithetic
terms, as a "tall, large, rough-looking man, in a journeyman
carpenter's uniform. Coarse, sanguine complexion; strong,
bristly, grizzled beard; singular eyes, of a semi-transparent,
indistinct light blue, and with that sleepy look that comes
when the lid rests half way down over the pupil; careless,

lounging gait." His companions—drivers, mechanics, laborers, ferryboat deckhands—epitomized "simple humanity." In the cabinet of Fowler & Wells, Walter Whitman had entered a wonderland of parabolic funhouse mirrors. He saw reflected in them the lineaments of "Walt Whitman, an American," "a man cohered out of tumult and chaos." Wrongheaded in theory and application, phrenology nonetheless provided Whitman with a structure of belief, a way of reasoning out glorious conclusions about the man and poet he became. In the building of a new self, Spurzheim's pseudoscience served him like the scaffoldings around the speculative houses he once put up in Brooklyn. In time he dismantled his phrenological staging and uprights and the new self stood unaided, but he never forgot its origins. "I know what [Oliver Wendell] Holmes said about phrenology," he joked toward the end of his life, "—that you might as easily tell how much money is in a safe feeling the knob on the door as tell how much brain a man has by feeling the bumps on his head: and I guess most of my friends distrust it—but you see I am very old fashioned—I probably have not got by the phrenology stage yet."

In 1855, when Whitman presented himself coatless and barenecked like "one of the roughs," his pelvis thrust foward, in the *Leaves of Grass* frontispiece, men of fashion dressed from head to toe like black tubes. Women of fashion resembled tea cozies, jam pots, and other gently rounded objects of manufacture—their breasts, buttocks, and legs were hidden under nearly 100 yards of gown, petticoat, and underclothing. In the name of health and public order the body had been officially banished from polite society and its external shape and structure denied. Popular theorists of the day, in particular Sylvester Graham (eponym of the delicious cracker), argued that one act of sexual intercourse was for a man the equivalent of losing forty ounces of blood—a fifth of his entire supply; this appalling statistic served as a warning that sexual over-indulgence—meaning more than once a month—could cause tuberculosis, convulsions, and even imbecilism, for sex withered the thinking organs of men, just as thinking withered the reproductive organs of women. Sex was a major disorder, even a catastrophe—it was a wonder the human race had lasted as long as it had.

"Touch me, touch the palm of your hand to my body as I pass," Whitman wrote. "Be not afraid of my body."

> If I worship one thing more than another it shall be the
>   spread of my own body, or any part of it,
> Translucent mould of me it shall be you!

No other poet of his century wrote about the body with such explicitness and joy, anatomizing it at rest and cataloging its parts, celebrating it in the act of love:

> Without shame the man I like knows and avows the deliciousness
>   of his sex,
> Without shame the woman I like knows and avows hers.

No other poet of his century paid such a continuing high price for his boldness: ostracism, ostentatious neglect, censorship, legal action, expulsion, banning in Boston. Emerson and others had urged him to tone down *Leaves of Grass* and he had refused, arguing that his poetry was organic and integral, that "the dirtiest book in all the world is the expurgated book," and besides, sex was the root of roots, the life beneath the life. In his *Education*, Henry Adams asked himself "whether he knew of any American artist who had ever insisted on the power of sex, as every classic has always done; but he could think only of Walt Whitman . . . All the rest had used sex for sentiment, never for force; to them, Eve was a tender flower, and Herodias an unfeminine horror. American art, like the American language and American education, was as far as possible sexless. Society regarded this victory over sex as its greatest triumph."

Now, a curiosity about the sex lives of other people is a perfectly natural thing, and we know from Lytton Strachey that discretion is not the better part of biography. And yet having followed Whitman to a point where he stands so admirably opposed to the sexual standards of Victorian America, we find ourselves in a quandary. Judged by his declared standards of candor, not to mention those of our era of total disclosure dictated by an as-yet unwritten Freedom of Sexual Information Act, we know practically nothing about what he "did," even though, as he tells us, he chronically "aches with amorous love." In contrast to Whitman, whose aches reminded D. H. Lawrence of a steam engine, it is tempting for us to believe Ralph Waldo Emerson had the sex drive of a day-old corpse. But Emerson had four acknowledged children. This means that we are able to make four more inferences about his intimate conduct than we can about the publicly excitable but ultimately covert Whitman.

Realizing the importance of such inferences, when he was seventy-one years old Whitman made an astounding claim in a letter to the English critic John Addington Symonds: "The writing and rounding of L[eaves] of G[rass] has been to me the reason-for-being, & life comfort. My life, young manhood, midage, time South, &c: have all been jolly, bodily, and probably open to criticism—Tho' always unmarried I have had six children—two are dead—One living southern grandchild, fine boy, who writes to me occasionally." The consensus among the members of Whitman's inner circle was that this newly revealed chapter in his life was pure moonshine, the children and grandchild (none of whom have ever surfaced) being the "delusion"—panicky, defensive, pathetic, senile, or self-aggrandizing—of a sick man who "was not exactly himself at times toward the last," as one of his friends said. But the main point is that all his life Whitman had fatherhood fantasies and that he wrote this letter out of exasperation, after having been chivied relentlessly by Symonds and other homosexual admirers in England to acknowledge the ultimate meaning of a number of his poems celebrating what the phrenologists called "adhesiveness," or manly love, or the love of comrades.

53 - The Naked Self and Other Problems

"Perhaps I don't know what it all means—perhaps never did know," Whitman once said about these poems, displaying a mixture of naivete and disingenuousness. "Maybe I do not know all my meanings." He described himself in one newspaper interview as "an old bachelor who never had a love affair," and then, having had second thoughts, angrily repudiated the interview. Constantly enriching the already scumbled surface of his history, he hinted at affairs with women in New York, Washington, and New Orleans, but he also acknowledged that the most intense relationships of his life were always with younger men, variously and anomalously lumped together as brothers, sons, comrades, lovers. On the documentary level the problem of accounting for Whitman's sexuality is magnified by his practice of laundering, editing, and revising his archives, altering the sequence of a cycle of love poems in order to obscure their narrative connection with each other, doctoring his notebooks by tearing out pages or by changing "him" to "her" and a man's initials to a number code. During his last twenty years Whitman contributed a substantial share to those pyres of paper and columns of smoke marking the trail of nineteenth-century authors who dreaded what biographers might find after they were dead and gone. One can't blame these fugitives—they knew that even the best-disposed biographies have to have an adversary or inquisitorial aspect if they are to arrive at any kind of truth. What is at stake here is not just invasion of privacy but the biographer's obligation to give Whitman himself the freedom he never had to pursue his recognition that love, of whatever sort it may be, was the root of roots in his life and poetry. "I think [Emanuel] Swedenborg was right," Whitman remarked, "when he said there was a close connection—a very close connection— between the state we call religious ecstasy and the desire to copulate. I find Swedenborg confirmed in all my experience. It is a peculiar discovery." To do this discovery justice requires a much longer narrative.

"I rubbed my eyes a little, to see if this sunbeam were no illusion," Emerson said after he read *Leaves of Grass* for the first time. It is the work, of course, that remains the paramount mystery or, in Whitman's word, "miracle." One does not try to explain a miracle but only to describe, with as much precision, credibility, and passion as possible, the moments and years preceding and following the miracle. The irreducible reality of literary lives may not be the naked self at all but the sum of a writer's public verbal acts and ecstasies with language. And as a corollary to this, the drama of literary biography may have less to do with stalking the naked self to its burrow than with the tensions between the familiar, shared life of human beings—making it, making out, making a go of it, making waves, making a name—and a vision so singular it deserves to be regarded with awe.

GEOFFREY WOLFF
Minor Lives

"It's interesting—things that are interesting interest me." In *Black Sun*, my biography of Harry Crosby, I judged his mother's declaration to be "scatterbrained." Now I'm not so sure. Shortly before the publication of that book several years ago, I received an apostrophe from a friend, a writer to whom I had sent a complimentary copy. He was generous with praise for this and that, but closed with a question friends and reviewers have asked many times since: "Why Crosby?" He even essayed, in a friendly way, to answer it: "Probably he was all that was left over."

Crosby was a Boston patrician schooled at St. Mark's and at Harvard. He was the nephew and godson of J.P. Morgan, served with the ambulance corps in France during World War I, married a Boston divorceé (creating a scandal) and decamped with her to Paris, where his bride changed her name from Polly to Caresse. They established the Black Sun Press, which published elegant books by Kay Boyle, Archibald MacLeish, Hart Crane, and others. Crosby wrote many, many poems, only a few of them not awful. He gambled, outraged his parents, drove recklessly, learned to fly, maintained serial affairs with beautiful women of several nationalities, and on December 10, 1929, at the Hotel des Artistes in New York, at the age of thirty-one he shot and killed the wife of another Boston patrician, and then himself, in a suicide compact. This grisly theater played the tabloids for a few days, and then citizens turned their attentions elsewhere. Crosby's widow fueled, without much success, the legend of her husband; Malcolm Cowley brought Crosby on stage to drop the curtain on *Exile's Return*. But otherwise, Harry Crosby—his life, work, and death—endured in the world's memory as a mere footnote to the cultural history of Americans in Paris in the twenties.

I learned about Crosby from Cowley's narrative fifteen years before I began to write about him. Simply: his story stuck in my mind. I searched libraries for more about Crosby, and something by him. I found his poems in rare-book rooms, and didn't like them. As little as I liked them, however, there was something about their badness—energy, will, a breathtaking ignorance of literary conceit—that also stuck in my mind. I found his journals, *Shadows of the Sun*, and was struck by their consistent, even obsessive, vision: Crosby lived every minute as though it were his last. He was reckless, indifferent to consequence. He was not brave; a brave man overcomes fear. He was fearless. He announced again and again, from the time he was twenty-two, that he would kill himself, choose his own means and moment to leave the table before he was full. He was a phenomenon, not exemplary. Cancer might be regarded as exemplary, while a lightning strike is phenomenal. Crosby was like a lightning strike, and he interested me.

The reviews of *Black Sun* were generous, most of them. The reviewer for *Time* magazine justly observed that since I regarded Crosby as "unique, he was not a proper symbol of anything." From this simple enough statement, the reviewer extrapolated a question: "What then is the point of inflating an interesting footnote to the dimensions of a sizable book? The answer, certainly is gossip." The *New Republic*, having judged *Black Sun* "an elegant book," concluded in the same sentence that it was a "pointless and disappointing one. Geoffrey Wolff doesn't claim anything for Harry Crosby; he knows that Harry was not a poet and that his life was neither Art nor artful." Christopher Lehmann-Haupt, in the *New York Times*, felt cheated: "In the end, we are somewhat disappointed. One is not especially uplifted to have enjoyed a three-ring circus of scandal and antisocial behavior . . . And though Mr. Wolff skillfully dismantles Malcolm Cowley's thesis that Harry Crosby's life and death were paradigmatic of the so-called Lost Generation . . . he doesn't offer much by way of explanation to replace it." When the book appeared in England it was reviewed by prominent people in prominent places at considerable length. After detailing the scandalous, glamorous, and sensational character of Crosby's life and death, the reviewer would typically ask: Who could care about such a man? Who would *write* about him?

(During my last year as an undergraduate, a friend and I sat in the dark, day after spring day, watching teenagers three inches high maneuver to fill the live lens on *American Bandstand*. Outside it was warm and sunny, and we sat watching with the windows shut and the curtains drawn. One afternoon I said to my friend, "Good God, what a way to put in hours!" I was watching *American Bandstand* and speaking of the rock 'n' rollers. I felt my friend look at the back of my neck. He said, "Yeah.")

Why Harry Crosby? *It's interesting—things that are interesting interest me.* It seemed to me in 1971 when I began work on a biography of Crosby that any story that had stuck to my memory fifteen years was trying to tell me something. Too, there was an unexplained mystery about his suicide: Why did he kill himself, wealthy, happily married, in love and loved back, young, in excellent health? Why didn't he leave a note? Did he murder the woman he shot, or did she choose to die with him? I did not know the answers to any of these questions and was eager to find them out.

I knew when I began that I would not introduce to the world a great lost poet, or even a good one. I knew that I was distrustful of theses of every kind, that everything in my experience ran counter to the generalizing impulse. I hoped, when I was done with Crosby, to understand a man, not to have unriddled the secret of Man. I hoped also to bring news, as the word news is the kinsman of *novel*. I had written three novels when I began *Black Sun*, and had an affection for the novelist's control of his world, the sense of a world poised to be made up whole and shaped. I knew when I began *Black Sun* that such control was Crosby's principle ambition, and the most consequential fact of his life: he sought to make himself over and up. He determined to translate himself from a Boston banker into a Great Poet by the agency of Genius. Genius he calculated to attain by the agency of Madness. He was utterly without a sense of metaphor, so that he willy-nilly enacted rather than imagined his progress from Harvard boy to surrealist. He *did* what gifted poets write. Thus, for him, suicide was neither an idea nor a figure of speech; it was a bullet in his head.

Harry Crosby was the willing prisoner of his announcement that he would control his end, die when and as he chose. The biographer is, of course, the prisoner of his subject's facts. For a biographer like myself, preoccupied with narrative design rather than the fabrication of an archive, the facts of certain kinds of lives are impediments. Let's pretend for a moment that *minor* and *major* accurately describe a distinction between human beings and their works: what kind of book can be written of a man or woman who has written major poems and lived a minor life, or died a minor death? Surely, in such an instance, the subject's work is what matters. The subject has subsumed in work the mess of his life.

In Crosby's case his life stood as so much material, so much documented material, and I was left with what seemed to me the enviable task of making something from it. Harry

Crosby walked the earth thinking of himself as a major poet in the making. He looked forward to the judgment of posterity, and made that judgment easy of access by saving every scrap of paper upon which he scribbled. But however lunatic his program for himself, his sense of place was not utterly in arrears, and when he shot himself he left no note, wisely apprehending that whatever paltry and infelicitous message such a note gave the world would be the last word the world would take from him. By not leaving a note, by leaving everything else—letters, notebooks, variants of poems, diaries, receipts, guest-books, photographs, scrap-books, report cards, passports—he seemed to invite such a history as I tried to write, such a collaboration.

Black Sun is indeed gossip, insofar as gossip is narrative. Some gossip is unsubstantiated, and some gossip is true. The gossip in Black Sun is substantiated hearsay. Like any biographer, I have passed along other people's mail, trafficked in rumor, eavesdropped on the conversations Crosby recorded in his notebooks, pried into school and college transcripts, gossiped with his surviving friends and relatives about him. I did this not because I labored under the delusion that Crosby was exemplary of good poets (or even bad poets, though I might have made a case for the symptoms he shared with other bad poets of his age). I never thought of him as standing for Harvard or Boston or Paris or the twenties or exiles or philanderers or gamblers or ambulance drivers. I was from the beginning less interested in his superficial similarities with his fellow men than his deep differences. I assumed those differences and left it to readers, whom I cannot pretend to know with such intimacy as I know Crosby and myself, to discover likenesses between Crosby's case and their own.

W.H. Auden's pugnacious essay about autobiography, "Hic et Ille," addresses the question of the unique case, the hermetic life. Midway through a progression of aphorisms, Auden's temper snaps: "Literary confessors are contemptible, like beggars who exhibit their sores for money, but not so contemptible as the public that buys their books." Calming himself somewhat, he quotes Cesare Pavese, putting him in italics: "*One ceases to be a child when one realizes that telling one's trouble does not make it any better.*" (Pavese, like Crosby, ceased to breathe when he ceased telling his trouble; their suicides were not their last, best pieces of work, they were evidence that there was no work left in them.) Auden's case against the literature of the single personality, the kind of thing that *Black Sun* means to be, the kind of thing my subsequent book means to be, builds to this heartfelt dogma: "Our sufferings and weaknesses, in so far as they are personal, *our* sufferings, *our* weaknesses, are of no literary interest whatsoever. They are only interesting in so far as we can see them as typical of the human condition. A suffering, a weakness, which cannot be expressed as an aphorism should not be mentioned."

Now, here's a surface to press against! I freely confess that I never calculated Crosby's confessions, as I articulated them, to incline toward the aphoristic, to build toward some generalizing trope, some "thesis" such as Lehmann–Haupt of the *Times* yearned to have in place of Malcolm Cowley's. It has been my experience as a reader that a strategy of connection and generalization is bound to fail. In fiction it produces flat characters, types whose accessories and quirks are designed only to reinforce conventional wisdom. As artless as the aphoristic impulse may be in fiction, in biography it is inhumane, filing the burred edges, the *interesting* burred edges, from a subject in order to fit him smoothly to the shape of other characters of his "type," to slip him like a greased key into the lock of received expectation. And in autobiography the impulse to generalize the writer's personal case is an unpardonable presumption: I cannot presume to know what experiences I share with you. If we share none, I can be certain you will find little of interest in my history, but I cannot design my history to satisfy *my* notion of *your* deepest yearnings.

These questions are not concluded in the purity of a vacuum, of course. Empirical data condition the biographer's apprehensions. When I told people in conversation about Harry Crosby—what he did rather than what he stood for—people seemed interested. As morally repugnant as it may be, the truth is that his suicide authenticated his life. It is awful to watch someone with good eyesight and all his senses on full alert walk with gravity and determination toward the edge of a precipice, and keep going. Had Crosby stopped at the edge, peered down, turned around and died in bed at eighty, I would not have written a book about him. I'm troubled by this fact; it is truly ghoulish, but I don't pretend not to understand it. My preoccupation, for better or worse, was with narrative, and without Crosby's suicide his narrative would have been shapeless, pointless.

I run counter in this assertion to the spirit of biography. The true biographer is above all a writer who receives facts and bravely accomodates them. If the biographer's subject writes a great book or passes a great law at the age of twenty-four, and thereafter lives a life of dwindling vision and intensity, dying at ninety-four, following ten years of senility, well, there you are, that's life, that's death. Crosby gave me a pretty arc, a life lived flat out, a death chosen as a fitting climax. Because he calculated his death's effects, I was left to judge the act's aesthetic value as well as its moral horror, and I welcomed the occasion to pipe up about something that interests me so deeply. Harry Crosby noted with approval the opinion of William James that when a man takes his own life "the fact consecrates him forever. Inferior to ourselves in this way or that, if yet we cling to life, and he is able to 'fling it away like a flower' as caring nothing for it, we account him in the deepest way our born superior."

That is, the question of suicide is interesting. Camus said, and I agree, that there is no question more interesting. And because Crosby's was uncomplicated by bad health, alcoholism, unrequited love, unpaid bills, old age or a disappointing Christmas, his suicide seemed on the face of it worth thinking and writing about.

Critics have distinguished between the Romantic and Augustan conventions in biography and autobiography. The Augustan impulse is exemplary (though not, probably, as Auden would have understood the term): it is an autobiography in two boxed volumes by a statesman, or a biography of a major author. It inclines toward the archival, the archeological. Joseph Blotner's *Faulkner: A Biography* is such an Augustan labor as I have in mind. William Gass has called this a "massive Egyptian work ... not so much a monument to a supremely gifted writer as it is the great man's grave itself, down which the biographer's piously gathered data drops like sheltering dirt ... " Gass has imagined the subject of such biography, a fellow named Feaster, whom he addresses, warning what the future will make of him: "It would mount in a museum your high school ring, wonder at your watch, your St. Christopher medal; and then your body, from dental crown and crew cut to appendix scar and circumcision, would become, as all enduring human matter does, abstract and general; you would not be a member any longer, but a species, a measure like the meter bar in Paris." The Romantic convention celebrates the member rather than the species, investigates the particular case. It is fundamentally autobiographical, and for better or worse my own work—I confess!—has tended toward it. During the editing process of *Black Sun*, about a man who died eight years before I was born, I was told many times, too many times, that my book had "too much Geoffrey Wolff in it." To the extent that the biographer's voice derails *his* narrative, or bullies his subject into submission, the biographer has botched his work. But to deny biography the signature of a style, the sound of a single voice rather than the crowd-noise of the species Biographer, seems perverse, artless, and servile.

Leon Edel has written that the art of biography "lies in the telling; and the telling must be of such a nature as to leave the material unaltered." I'm not certain that any telling can leave material unaltered; point of view alters data, dogma deforms it, and putative objectivity (the absence of a point of view) confuses it. The best the biographer can hope for is what Lytton Strachey demanded of himself, that he ". . . lay bare the facts of his case, as he understands them."

Where are the facts of a "minor" case to come from? I expected to learn about Crosby in Paris, among his surviving contemporaries. I traveled to France, and enjoyed France, but I learned nothing there about the man I had promised my publisher I would write about. I returned to America chastened, and anxious. A kind man led me to a book titled *American Literary Manuscripts* that lists major holdings of letters and manuscripts by our libraries. This directed me to the New York Public Library, which in fact had no Crosby papers, and to Brown University, which did. At Brown were some letters and photographs, and many volumes of notebooks, the raw material from which *Shadows of the Sun* was formed.

At Brown I learned that huge numbers of papers belonging to Crosby's widow Caresse had been purchased by Southern Illinois University in Carbondale, and these I was allowed to examine during several week-long visits. Here were letters to Crosby from D.H. Lawrence, James Joyce, Archibald MacLeish, lady friends, his parents and relatives. Here were notebooks in which Crosby recorded in close detail the most intimate aspects of his life. By checking his notebook entries against letters to his wife and mother and father, I soon learned that he was a relentless truth-teller, and that I could trust him. I also realized that his short life was so amply documented that it left little to surmise, save the ruling question of his life: his death.

I resolved to take advantage of this documentation to the fullest, weaving the raw facts of his history through my text as artfully as I knew how, using the dialogue he had so thoughtfully preserved. I had no wish to be accused of having

"novelized" my biography, and I knew that without supporting apparatus to identify the sources of the data I presented, I
would not, should not, be taken on faith. Whenever a bit is
taken from here, and another bit from there, sometimes in
violation of chronology, the synthesis is partial, even
tendentious, and I wanted my readers to have access to the
exact parts that comprise *Black Sun's* whole. So I borrowed
from Barbara Tuchman and others the device of placing notes
at the back of the book, with references to sources identified
by the initial and final words of the passage on a given page. In
this way I freed myself to leave my narrative unmolested by
justifications and attributions.

The following passage from page 278 of *Black Sun* gives a
sense of the kind of narrative synthesis the biographer
employs. Here, for the sake of illustration, I identify with
intrusive footnotes where the scraps came from:

> The day before Harry, Caresse and Constance sailed for New York
> on the *Mauretania*, the Crosbys had some people to tea at 19 rue de
> Lille: Ambassador Joseph Grew, Alex and Sylvia Steinert, the
> Crouchers, Goops and a few others.[1] The next afternoon, November
> 16, several of these, together with Eugene Jolas, saw them off with a
> party on the railway platform in Paris.[2] As soon as they boarded at
> Cherbourg, a telegram was delivered to Harry. The message was
> terse—YES—but to him not cryptic. It was signed by the Sorceress.[3]
> Three days later, sitting with Constance in the smoking room during
> a storm[4]—both at sea and with Caresse, who was sulking in her
> stateroom, jealous of Constance[5]—and reading *Beating the Stock
> Market*,[6] he was brought another radiogram.
> "I guess this must be from my girl in Boston," he told Constance.
> "Oh, Harry," she said, "I do hope you aren't going to get mixed up
> with that girl again. She's married, and you aren't really in love with
> her anyway."
> "I love three people," he replied. "Caresse, you, and Josephine."[7]

> 1. The names of the Crosby's visitors, and the fact that there was
> such a party, came from a guest book among papers at Southern
> Illinois University.
> 2. I know that Eugene Jolas said goodbye to the Crosbys from his
> unpublished memoir, which his widow let me read in Paris.

3. The telegram from "the Sorceress" is among Crosby's papers at Brown University, and I surmise that it was delivered in person to Harry by an instruction on the envelope: "Deliver to stateroom."
4. That there was a violent storm during their passage I learned from New York newspapers on microfilm in the annex of the New York Public Library.
5. That Caresse sulked, jealous, in her stateroom while Crosby passed time with Constance, I learned from *Shadows of the Sun*.
6. That Crosby was reading *Beating the Stock Market* during the afternoon this second telegram was delivered I learned from his meticulously annotated reading record, among his papers at Southern Illinois University.
7. The conversation between Harry and Constance was duplicated in a letter from Constance to Caresse following Harry's suicide.

In addition to twenty-eight pages of notes, an annotated bibliography and a chronology (which liberated me to move back and forth through the text in time, following where topics rather than the calender led), I included an index, so that readers could locate the "major" figures who intersected my minor subject. I interviewed as many people as I could find (and would talk with me)—more than a hundred—but not until I had soaked myself in Crosby's documents. More than forty years had passed since his death, and I interviewed people called upon to reach back in memory more than half a century. A few had astounding recall: Edward Weeks and Archibald MacLeish could attach episodes to dates accurate within a tolerance of a week or two. But for the most part the utility of these interviews was to observe in which ways memory had altered Crosby into a figure of legend or contempt, to watch the critical faculty seep through the compost pile of all those years. Finally, when I caught myself giving rather than taking information, when I spent more time telling Crosby's friends and kinsmen what they *really* knew about him than asking what they knew, it was time to lock my study door from the inside, and begin writing.

My next book is called *The Duke of Deception*. It is ... what? Biography, sort of. Autobiography, I guess. On its account I stopped asking questions and began writing, not because I finally knew all I could know, but because there was so little really to know. The book is about my father—Arthur "Duke" Wolff—a "minor" subject if ever there was one, but a major father to me. He is remembered, and not fondly, by hornswoggled bankers, unpaid merchants, and police and prison officers of the four quadrants of the United States. And by me. He died before my children met him, and the book I have written about him, and my childhood with him, is for them.

Like *Black Sun*, *The Duke of Deception* begins with its subject's end. These are minor characters, after all, and to begin with their beginnings, with births, would beg much of a reader's curiosity. More important, I don't like books that tease, and I have tried to tell stories whose suspense is of character rather than episode: *Here's what Harry Crosby did; let me try to show why.*

What Crosby said he'd do he did, exactly, which is why he interests me. What my father said he had done, he had not done. I grew up in a family in which much was suggested and little was explained, in which misapprehensions were exploited, lovingly manured. My father was a Jew, and said he was not. My father said he was a Groton and Yale and Skull & Bones man, and he was not. My father said he had inherited a huge fortune, but he did not. Everything that mattered most to me I learned late, and in a rush. And that is how I learned that my father would not live forever.

The death of a father is the crucial natural event in a man's life. It changes everything, at once, and in a way that no one can anticipate. Suddenly there is no more becoming; everything is being, unwinding. A man imagines his own children's response to this calamity in their lives and shudders to know that the experience of a father's death is a deliverance as well as a blow. There is no further need to explain, to apologize. The surviving son is dreadfully, wonderfully free.

When I turned twenty-one my father gave me a heavy gold signet ring that he said had been in our family many years. In fact, I later learned, the ring had been fabricated according to his design in Hollywood and had never been paid for. Beneath some lions rampant on a field of fleurs–de–lis is a motto, engraved backwards to come out right on a red wax seal. It says *NULLA VESTIGIUM RETORSIT*, and my father told me this means *don't look back*. In fact it means, if it means anything, *not a trace left behind*.

Well, I'm left behind, and my sons are left behind, too. And the only way I know to deal with that intractable fact is to write about it, to write about my father for my sons. I have been writing about him since I began to write, usually in anger. By the time I began *The Duke of Deception* all the anger seemed dissipated. My father left many victims, and for a long time I numbered myself among them. I was ashamed of him, and hated him for the lies he had told me, especially for the lie he told most insistently, that only truth can set us free, that the only way we could confirm our love for each other was to tell each other the truth.

I decided, when my father died, that only the truth could convey to my children the experience of having been my father's son, and that it was important that they have a record of that experience. I was mindful, and am more mindful now, that the truth, as it is regarded by scientists and philosophers, is beyond my reach. I was nurtured by lies about my history, and some of these can never be unraveled. Memory is selective, and the iron principle of life as well as narrative is the partiality of point of view.

But there is a kind of truth that should be within reach of a participant in the events of his narrative, however difficult that truth may be to grasp. It is the kind of truth that can be won by a willingness to distinguish between what a writer feels he should have felt at a particular moment, and what he really felt. As I learned to make that distinction, uneasily, I learned again what I had forgotten, that I had had in many ways a happy childhood, that it had been fun to be my father's son.

I knew as little about the facts of his history when I began as I had known of the facts of Harry Crosby's, and when I was finished I had fewer facts about him than about Crosby. (Though I knew him a world better.) I began with the conviction that lives can be revealed only by their enactments, a conviction deepened by my experience of Harry Crosby. I would not put my father on the couch, pretend to fathom his motives. I would instead reveal his comings and goings, his doings. As I could not with Crosby, I would try to give the sense of him, how he filled space in a room, the key and range and timbre of his speech, his smell of leather and tobacco and silver polish.

I had to dig deep for his facts. There was no family archive, no chest in the attic. We had moved often and abruptly, traveling light to keep more than a rope's-length ahead of the posse. There were police records, and I knew that my father had been born in Hartford, the son of a surgeon, he said. For once he said true, and by writing hospitals and medical licensing bureaus I began to accumulate a record of my grandparents, helped by a couple of cousins, one of whom took me to the graveyard where I learned the death dates that led me to obituaries.

I found my father's record at Deerfield, where he had been a student, and from which he had been expelled. One school led to another, and in their records was the history of a bad boy, but not as bad as his father thought. In the school files were violent, hectoring, whining letters about my father from my grandfather, hugely unhappy about my father's petty vices. I heard from the grandfather I never met the stridency of rhetoric that my father turned against me when he was drunk, and I felt the vice shut on him, as it now and then seemed to have shut on me. I began to experience the connection Auden calls for, but it was, of course, merely personal, a closed circuit from a father to a son to his son, by way of a conductor—a book—back to the first father.

I knew by now, having anatomized Harry Crosby's will to change himself from one kind of character to another, that a mask is often more interesting than the "authentic" character it disguises, and I felt prepared to give my father his givens, to judge them as I had tried to judge Crosby's suicide, aesthetically as well as morally. In plain words, I was less interested in what my father *was*, in whether he was in fact a Skull & Bones man, than in what he wished people to believe he was.

Given my interest, how can I concern myself with the world's judgment of major and minor subjects? Surely we know enough to realize that celebrity cannot enhance an autobiographer's claim to a reader's attention. In the kind of book it has been my ambition to write, the work itself stands as the writer's bid for a place in the world, as the writer's subject's bid for a place in the world. If I have done my work well someone will say, reading it, *I wish I had known that Duke*, by which the reader will mean not that he would have liked to have met a Skull & Bones man, but that he would have liked to hear my father lie about being a Skull & Bones man.

Writing is not therapy, but it can heal, translating vague, unarticulated pain into narrative. Narrative demands calculation and proportion, and the critical faculty that drives any comely narrative insists that character—if it is to connect, if it has the hope of connecting—be born into the narrative as into the world, selfish, but not alone. Character in narrative is interesting only in relation to other characters in narrative. The ubiquitous "I" may in fact be a solipsist, but no solipsist ever drove a good narrative alone; his effect on others must be registered, and the effect on him of others, too. Children think of themselves as alone in the world. At least I did; narrative restored my case to its deeper reality, a process of strophe and antistrophe, commerce, community, a family, the annihilation of such modifying titles as "major" and "minor."

William Gass has located the peril at the heart of autobiography, the insane sense that one alone counts: "The lively force and narcissistic drama of one's situation, like a passion or a toothache for which the world shuts shop, so only one's wound is open, only one's pain is beating, easily leads to the conviction that the rush of lust through the loins, the ache, the ear which won't stop ringing, are universal conditions of consciousness ... "

So, with Auden, one hopes that one's case will touch others. But how to connect? Not by calculation, I think, not by the assumption that in the pain of my toothache, or my father's, or Harry Crosby's, I have discovered a "universal condition of consciousness." One may merely know that no one is alone and hope that a singular story, as every true story is singular, will in the magic way of some things apply, connect, resonate, touch a major chord.

ALFRED KAZIN
The Self as History:
Reflections on Autobiography

"Every man has reminiscences which he would not tell to everyone, but only to his friends. He has other matters in his mind which he would not reveal even to his friends, but only to himself, and that is secret. But there are other things which a man is afraid to tell even to himself, and every decent man has a number of such things stored away in his mind. The more decent he is, the greater the number of such things in his mind . . . A true autobiography is almost an impossibility. . . . man is bound to lie about himself."

Dostoevsky: Notes From Underground

"Whoever undertakes to write a biography binds himself to lying, to concealment, to flummery, and even to hiding his own lack of understanding, since biographical material is not to be had, and if it were it could not be used. Truth is not accessible; mankind does not deserve it, and wasn't Prince Hamlet right when he asked who would escape a whipping if he had his deserts?"

Sigmund Freud

"We are all special cases."

Albert Camus

I do not know what "autobiography" is; the genre changes with each new example. What I have tried to write in *A Walker in the City, Starting Out in the Thirties, New York Jew*, is personal history, a form of my own influenced by the personal writings of Emerson, Thoreau, Whitman. Its passion and beat come from my life in history, recorded since I was a boy in notebooks that I value not for their facts but for the surprise I attain by writing to myself and for myself. "I write for myself and strangers," said Gertrude Stein. The strangers, dear reader, are an afterthought.

In my experience, Americans sooner or later bring any discussion around to themselves. The American writers with whom, more than any others, I have lived my spiritual life, tend to project the world as a picture of themselves even when they are not writing directly about themselves. No doubt this has much to do with the emphasis on the self in America's ancestral Protestantism. Theology in America tends to be Protestant. The self remains the focal point of American literary thinking. From Jonathan Edwards to Hemingway we are confronted by the primitive and unmediated self arriving alone on the American strand, then battling opposing selves who share with us only the experience of being an American.

The deepest side of being an American is the sense of being like nothing before us in history—often enough like no one else around us who is not immediately recognized as one of our tradition, faith, culture, profession. *"What do you do, bud?"* is the poignant beginning of American conversation? "Who are *you?* What am I to expect from *you?"* put into history's language, means that I am alone in a world that was new to begin with and that still feels new to me because the experience of being so *much* a "self"—constantly explaining oneself and telling one's own story—is as traditional in the greatest American writing as it is in a barroom.

What is being talked about is inevitably oneself as a creature of our time and place, the common era that is the subject of history. Every American story revolving around the self, even Henry Miller as a derelict in Paris, is a story of making it against a background symbolically American. Miller made it to Paris after years of being an indistinguishable big-city nobody. In Paris this American nobody wrote himself up as somebody, a symbol of the free life. The point of the story—as it was for Ben Franklin arriving in Philadelphia, Emerson crossing "a bare common" in ecstasies at his newly recognized spiritual powers, Whitman nursing the helpless wounded soldiers in the Civil War hospitals, Henry Adams in awe of the dynamo at the 1900 Paris exposition, E. E. Cummings observing his fellow prisoners in *The Enormous Room*, Hemingway in Parisian cafes writing about his boyhood in Upper Michigan—is that he is making a book out of it, a great book, an exemplary tale of some initiating and original accomplishment that could have been imagined only in an American book. The background seems to say that although the creative spirit is peculiarly alone in America, it is alone *with* America. Here the self, the active, partisan, acquisitive self, born of society, is forever remaking itself, but not in the direction that Keats called "a vale of soul-making."

We tend to emphasize the self as a creature of history and

history as a human creation. Even Emerson, the last truly religious, God-oriented writer we have had, the last to believe that the world exists entirely *for* the individual and that "Nature is meant to serve," even Emerson wobbles on the ultimate existence of the individual soul, feels easier with a universal cloud cover called the "Oversoul" than he does with the traditional religious soul in God's keeping, i.e., the soul as the human index and analog of a spiritual world. What Emerson is talking about in *Nature, The American Scholar, The Divinity School Address*, is the "active soul" of the writer as a teacher to humanity. Emerson, whose doctrine gave full faith and comfort to rugged individualism, is a great modern writer not yet altogether secularized. He despises fiction, calls poet and prophet interchangeable terms, *preaches* the necessity to leave the church behind and find God in one's "immeasurable mind." Yet Emerson was so typically double-sighted that he also wrote the first great American book on the old country— *English Traits*. How strange that the same man in his journals as well as in his famous lectures on everything at large, nevertheless plays the preacher. What he habitually says is that he has taken himself out of the church, out of formal Christianity, in order to prove that one man, by himself, can be a bridge to divine truth.

And that man is you, my fellow American. You can become as great an artist in words as Ralph Waldo Emerson: All you have to do is become a church to yourself and preach from your own immortal genius. July 15, 1838, a Sunday evening before the senior class at Divinity College, Harvard:

> And now, my brothers, you will ask, What in these desponding days can be done by us? . . .
> Wherever a man comes, there comes revolution. The old is for slaves. When a man comes, all books are legible, all things transparent, all religions are forms. . . . Yourself a newborn bard of the Holy Ghost, cast behind you all conformity and acquaint man at first hand with Deity . . . Live with the pleasure of the immeasurable mind.

America itself seemed immeasurable in opportunity: "Nature," which meant everything outside of man, existed to serve man on this continent. An American armed with the primacy of the self, can do anything. Especially in words. Like Emerson, he can invent a religion just for free spirits and call it literature. Like Thoreau, he can turn a totally lonely life, the death of his beloved brother John, his penny-pinching, lung-destroying, graphite-owning family, into the most beautiful prose fable we have of man perfectly at home with nature. Like Whitman, who took self-revelation as his basic strategy, he can propose a whole new self—which for millions he has become. Whitman, who wrote a great book in the form of a personal epic, compelled and still compels many readers to believe him not only the desperado poet he was but one of the supreme teachers of a troubled humanity. And then in prose, this worldly failure used the Civil War as an abundant backdrop to his picture of himself as tending the wounded soldiers, an American St. Francis who reincarnated himself as a poet, thanks to war and the assassination on Good Friday of his beloved Lincoln. Henry Adams in the *Education* reverses his loneliness as a widower, his isolation as an historical imagination, into the exquisite historical myth of a Hamlet kept from his rightful kingship—a Hamlet too good for Denmark—a Hamlet who nevertheless knew everybody in the world worth knowing—a Hamlet who finally turned the tables on science, the only knowledge worth having. Adams's last superlative myth is a world that in the twelfth century stood still to worship the Virgin but in the twentieth is racing madly, whirling into outer space in its lust to satisfy Emerson's "immeasurable mind"—intellectual power.

Henry James in his autobiographical prefaces to his collected works and in that staggering personal reverie over what the New World has become, *The American Scene*, showed what mastership over the visible world the literary American self could attain. William James in the personal testimony that is among the most valuable sections of that Emersonian manual in spiritual self-help, *The Varieties Of Religious Experience*, showed—in the classic pattern of Protestant autobiography from *Pilgrim's Progress* to John Woolman's *Journal*—that a basic function of such writing is to cure oneself of guilt and self-division.

William James was not the first psychiatrist in America, though he was the student and colleague of those at Harvard who helped to inaugurate this still indefinable therapy. But Dr. James was a genius—it was his best gift—at putting himself together again, in words. To heal thyself is a classic reason for a worried man's becoming a physician, especially a psychiatrist. But no psychologist to my knowledge confessed his divided self so eloquently as did William James; no other has so clearly erected a whole system of *belief* to deal with it. James is Emerson's true successor at the end of the century. Emerson never confessed to doubts and was, as Henry James, Sr., said bitterly, a man impossible to get hold of, "without a handle." William James more than anyone in his time understood the American idea that religion helps us shed our sickness, especially in books.

Hemingway was to say that the only psychiatrist *he* needed was a Smith-Corona. But Hemingway, like Saul Bellow in our day, used his own experience obsessively in the form of fiction. So Hemingway kept up the pose to the end that he was invulnerable, famous for "grace under pressure," until the gun in his mouth made it too late for him to admit that his public pose was one great fiction. For the nonfiction writer, as I can testify, personal history is directly an effort to find salvation, to make one's own experience come out right. This is as true of Edmund Wilson in his many autobiographical essays and notebooks as it is of James Baldwin, Malcolm X, Claude Brown. It is even true of straight autobiography by fiction writers. Hemingway's account of his apprenticeship to letters in Paris, *A Moveable Feast*, is an effort to save himself by recovering an idyllic past. Fiction is never simply autobiography—not when it is written by a genuine novelist. The autobiographical impulse in fiction takes the form of satire, burlesque, grandiose mythology, as in *Moby Dick*. It often mocks the hero and the novel form itself; it generally becomes something altogether different from autobiography by introducing so many other leading characters.

Even the most lasting autobiographies—St. Augustine, Rousseau, Henry Adams—tend to be more case histories limited to the self, as its own history to begin with, then the self as the history of a particular moment and crisis in human history. Saul Bellow has written only one novel, *The Victim*, in which he has not sat for a leading character. Sammler and Charles Citrine, Herzog, and even Henderson, represent Bellow in various stages of his life, different moods, different wives. But there are so many other people and points of interest in his novels, like the frolicsome portrait of the poet Delmore Schwartz in *Humboldt's Gift*, that it is clear that what makes the human comedy balance out right is the creative process for this self-renewing novelist, not Bellow's own history.

Still, wholly personal documents like Whitman's *Specimen Days*, Adams's *Education*, Conrad Aiken's *Ushant*, Malcolm X's *Autobiography*, can be more lasting than many a novel. What preserves such books is the news they bring us of history in a new form. In every notable case of this form, from Franklin's *Autobiography* to Richard Wright's *Black Boy* and Frederick Exley's *A Fan's Notes*, we have the epic of personal struggle, a situation rather than a plot. The writer turns himself into a representative sinner or Christian or black or Jew—in Exley's case a comically incurable drunk.

This person, we say to ourselves as we encounter Franklin arriving in Philadelphia, has *lived* history. These are people recounting their fame. Here is Edward Gibbon: "It was at Rome, on the 15th of October 1764, as I sat musing amid the ruins of the Capitol, while the barefooted friars were singing vespers in the temple of Jupiter, that the idea of writing the decline and fall of the city first started to my mind." But Gibbon's book is all about how important he was; he is incapable of making fun of himself. It is not from his innocently pompous memoirs that we learn that the great historian as a member of Parliament from a rotten borough fell asleep during the debates on the American Revolution. One can *live* history in a quite different way, as witness Franklin's comic account of himself walking up Market Street, carrying two rolls, eating a third, and seeing his future wife "when she standing at the door saw me, and thought I made as I certainly did, a most awkward appearance."

To "live" history is not of course to command it, or even one's fate in life. To live history is to express most memorably a relationship to the past, to a particular setting, to a moment, sometimes even to a particular set of buildings, as Henry James does so vibrantly in that travel book of sheer genius, *The American Scene*, where buildings are talking to one another because James's mind is so busily interrogating them.

My favorite example of history-to-the-life is Henry Adams's account of being taken as a boy to Washington. He has already told us in many indirect and delightful ways that he is the grandson and great-grandson of presidents. He is staying with his grandmother, the widow of John Quincy Adams:

> Coming down in the early morning from his bedroom in his grandmother's house—still called the Adams building—in F Street and venturing outside into air reeking with the thick odor of the catalpa trees, he found himself on the earth-road, or village street, with wheel tracks meandering from the colonnade of the Treasury hard by, to the white marble columns and fronts of the Post Office and Patent Office which faced each other in the distance, like white Greek temples in the abandoned gravel-pits of a deserted Syrian city.

This is a passage of historical music. The key words are sacred names, as Proust said of Combray, as Gibbon rang the litany of historical names in the great passage enumerating Rome, the ruins of the Capitol, barefooted friars singing vespers in the temple of Jupiter. Adams is also rendering the art of history by locating himself as a boy of twelve wandering from the house of "Madame President" through the ancient sleepy undistinguished unfinished Washington of 1850. Unlike Gibbon's Rome, all in ruins, Adams's Washington is seen by *us* as the powerful America of the future, but strangely ignorant of its future as we see the earth-road, the village streets, wheeltracks. But note that the Treasury has a Greek colonnade and, a most rewarding detail, the white marble columns and fronts of the Post Office and Patent Office in the distance face each other like white Greek temples in the abandoned gravel-pits of a deserted Syrian city. The innocently pompous all-marble Washington of the future, where Adams wrote this passage in 1905 sitting in his great house just across Lafayette Square from the White House, must contend in our minds with the beautifully supple historical imagination of Adams the great historian picturing Syria forgotten in the ruins of the Roman Empire.

When Adams wrote this passage America had just acquired, out of the goodness of its heart, the Philippines, Puerto Rico, Cuba. Adams's sometime friend Theodore Roosevelt, whom he amusedly tolerated as a gentleman from his own set (he thought the president insane), was enjoying the presidency with unholy zest. The moment had already come at the great Paris exposition of 1900 when Adams discovered that his "historical back" was broken by the sight of the dynamo:

> The planet itself seemed less impressive, its old-fashioned, deliberate, annual or daily revolution, than this huge wheel, revolving within arm's length at some vertiginous speed, and barely murmuring— scarcely humming an audible warning to stand a hair's breadth further for respect of power—while it would not wake the baby lying close against its frame. Before the end, one began to pray to it; inherited instinct taught the natural expression of man before silent and infinite force. . . .

This is the self living history as its own fate. The barely

murmuring dynamo will turn soon into the rocket, Adams into Norman Mailer at Cape Kennedy awed by the towering hangar built to house the moon rocket. The mountebank in the White House, Theodore Roosevelt, will become the succession of presidents after Vietnam unable to halt their own powerlessness. History as our own fate is what the grandiose theoretical last chapters of the *Education* have to teach us. And that is the deepest meaning of "autobiography," historically considered. Adams in Washington, 1850, yields to Adams in Washington, 1900, to ourselves in Washington and New York in 2000. The infinite universe mocks the American belief that its power is constant and growing, surrounded by empires without our ancient belief in the goodness of all people brought up under constitutional democracy.

Walt Whitman is another great example of the self living history—first as a mere spectator; then as our common fate, history as the ultimate explanation of our individual fortunes in life. In *Song of Myself* Whitman wrote of the historical visions he painted of America at mid-century—*"I am the man, I suffer'd, I was there."* In his great diary of the Civil War, *Specimen Days*, Whitman describes himself going down to Washington to look for his brother George, wounded in the second battle of Bull Run. What Whitman does not say is that he was at his lowest ebb as poet and man. *Leaves of Grass* had failed, he really had nothing to occupy himself with at the moment, and he must have had an instinct that the war would be one of those historical tragedies in which the rejected of history find their souls again, in which the epics of the race are reborn.

Early in *Specimen Days* Whitman describes the beaten Federal soldiers in retreat lying along the streets of Washington. Only Whitman would have caught the peculiar poignance of the contrast between the marble Capitol and the helpless, often neglected suffering in what was now a very confused capital. The most splendid instance of Whitman's eye picking out such historical ironies is the description of the wounded soldiers lying in the Patent Office:

A few weeks ago the vast area of the second story of that noblest of Washington buildings was crowded close with rows of sick, badly wounded and dying soldiers. They were placed in three very large apartments. I went there many times. It was strange, solemn, and with all its features of suffering and death, a sort of fascinating sight. . . . Two of the immense apartments are filled with high and ponderous glass cases, crowded with models in miniature of every kind of utensil, machine, or invention it ever entered into the mind of man to conceive; and with curiosities and foreign presents. . . . It was indeed a curious scene, especially at night when lit up. The glass cases, the beds, the forms lying there, the gallery above, and the marble pavement underfoot. . . .

Whitman does not neglect to tell us at the end of this description of the Patent Office that the wounded soldiers have now been all removed. There *was* an historical moment; he was there. Just in time to record fully the typical American contrast between our technical genius and what war does. Whitman was not a soldier, not even a real nurse. History may well wonder if he gave as much to the soldiers as they gave him. They made possible his great poems and prose of the war. But there is present in *Specimen Days* and in the cycle of war poems, *Drum-Taps*, a kind of historical light or atmosphere that is extraordinary. It is a quality one finds only in the greatest books—from the *Iliad* to *War and Peace*—that show history itself as a character. A certain light plays on all the characters, the light of what we call history. And what is history in this ancient sense but the commemoration of our common experience, the unconscious solidarity of a people celebrated in the moments of greatest stress, as the Bible celebrates over and again history as the common experience of the race, from creation to redemption?

But something new has entered into twentieth-century experience. We no longer identify ourselves *with* history. Joyce's Stephen Dedalus said, "History is the nightmare from which I am trying to awaken." History since 1914 has become for the "educated classes" of the West not so much a memory as a threat. This may be one reason for the marked failure of "history" to awaken enthusiasm or even much intellectual curiosity among the young. To have a sense of history one must consider *oneself* a piece of history. Although our age will be remembered most of all for the endless multiplication of technological innovation and scientific information, the "feel" of the present—at least to the white middle class that still writes its history as the history of the world—is that history is out of control, beyond all the prophecies and calculations made for it in the nineteenth century, when the organization of industrial society was plainly the pattern of the future. Hence the unconscious despair of people whose first legend is the city of peace built on a hill, a new world to be born, a new man to be made.

But to the others, who are just arising in history and for whom history is their effort alone, the self knows history only as nemesis and liberation from oppression. Hence, in our immediate culture we get more and more a view of literature as political rhetoric. Imaginative literature even in our privileged society is now so much under the pressure of journalism, documentary, the media, the daily outrage and atrocity, and above all unconscious mass fright, that autobiography of one kind or another, often the meanest travel report through contemporary life, has become all too fashionable, omnipresent.

On every hand I seem to see people saying *I am the man, I got the story first, I was there.* Even that miserable schemer who tape-recorded himself out of the presidency had no higher aim than to write a best-seller called *Nixon as History.* The public gets more and more submissive to instant history. Looking at the endless news reports on television, we resemble savages cowering from the storm in their caves, waiting on the gods to decide our fate. Society, as we draw to the end of our century, resembles the primitive idea of nature as reward or punishment. The man on the spot may only be a ventriloquist's dummy, like most news commentators, reading what he has been given to read. But literature essentially does nothing different when it appeals, as our most gifted writers do, only to the public experience of politics, the moon voyage, the political assassination, the seeming irreconcilability of the sexes.

The real problem for "personal history" now is how to render this excess of outer experience as personal but not private experience. This is the feminine tradition, and women writers know better than men how to turn the glib age of incessant reportage back into personal literature. But there is at the same time so clamorous a cry of personal weakness, so much confessional poetry and fiction, that I ask myself, as a "personal historian," what the spell is on all of us—not least our readers. For of course Plath, Lowell, Berryman, Rich, Olsen, Duncan, Ginsberg, Sexton, Wakoski would not have written such texts, would not be the stars of the classroom nowadays if there were not so many readers who seem to read no poetry and prose that is not confessional, who demand that literature be about the confessional self—an invitation to become confessional themselves.

Does this mean that the theme I began with, the autobiographer as a triumph over his own life, has changed into the self-proclaimed disaster? Of course not. Confession is possible, even popular. We live in a society whose standards of personal conduct have been mocked by all our recent presidents, to say nothing of our leading corporation executives. The open lust for political advantage over human rights and belief in our American superpowers have made breakdown and confession, Vietnam, Watergate and investigation, a pattern of our time.

Erik Erikson says that all confession is an effort to throw off a curse. Guilt seems more endemic than it ever did. It is certainly more popular. Why? No doubt it makes possible a confessional literature that is self-dramatizing in the absence of moral authority. At the same time the dramatization of the self in American literature goes back to a very old theme.

How well have I made out? What am I to think of *my* life, all things considered? Could it have been any different? Let us not deceive ourselves: Each person, especially in this historically still most hopeful of countries, is constantly making up the progress report of his life, and knows that in this respect everyone we know, love, and hate, everyone to whom we have ever been tied, shares our interests exactly—this life, my life, this time . . .

So the anxious but somehow thrivingly preoccupied self, in a culture where personal fortune and happiness are more real than God has become even to many believers, cannot help connecting himself with people like himself in this period, with a history that betrays the most intimate passions. Once gods of the earth, presidents now seem all too much like ourselves. More and more the sexes are compelled to admit that men and women—alas!—are more alike than we had dreamed, egotists before anything else. Everywhere we turn we seem to be within the same bedroom walls, under pressure from the same authorities. Hence, not equality but *identity* becomes the condition of life as we get mashed into shape by the same corporations, shopping plazas, ranch houses, mass universities, television programs, instant replay of the same public atrocities.

In all this the self becomes freely articulate about itself, recognizing a *psychological* bond with other selves that is negative. Every confession becomes a progress report of the most intense interest to others. And if the confession is an attempt to ward off a curse, writing it out is also a boast: To be able to write one's life, to make one's way successfully through so many ghosts, between so many tombs, is indeed a boast.

All I have to boast about is that I have at least tried to express my life. I have been saved by language. My sixty years have been lived directly *and* symbolically in the storm centers of the twentieth century. Nothing seems more remote than the illusion of security and tranquillity as the century accelerates the violence and nihilism that have marked all our lives since 1914-1918 showed that the concentrated power of modern weapons can be even more suicidal than private despair.

Yet I believe that history exists, that it is still meaningful, and that we can read our fate in the book of history. That gives me the courage to write. To write is in some way to cut the seemingly automatic pattern of violence, destructiveness, and death wish. To write is to put the seeming insignificance of human existence into a different perspective. It is the need, the wish, and, please God, the ability, to reorder our physical fate by mental means, a leap of the imagination, an act of faith. Wallace Stevens once wondered in an essay whether it is not "the violence within that protects us from the violence without." The "violence within" is the effort to make a mental construct that shall hang together—that shall be within the inner landscape a seamless and uninterruptable web—that can prove, as Henry James said, that "the whole truth about anything is never told; we can only take what groups together."

Violence is distinguished by gaps, discontinuities, inconsistency, confusion condensed into power—but no less blind and chaotic for that. The life of mere experience, and especially of history as the supposedly total experience we ridiculously claim to know, can seem an inexplicable series of unrelated moments. But language, even when it is most a mimicry of disorder, is distinguished from violence, atrocity, deceit, by relating word to word, sentence to sentence, thought to thought—man to this final construct on a page— always something different from mere living.

So that is why I write, to reorder an existence that man in the mass will never reorder for me. Even autobiography is a necessary stratagem to gain something more important than itself. By the time experience is distilled enough through our minds to set some particular thing down on paper, so much unconscious reordering has gone on that even the naive wish to be wholly "truthful" fades before the intoxication of line, pattern, form.

Stephen Crane said that art is a child of pain. Existence is itself an anxious matter for many Americans in the twentieth century precisely because the material power is greatest in this country; we have had the greatest illusion of control. And so the disappointment and anger are greater still. In the writing of our time and place, one sees a greater questioning, philosophical and moral rootlessness, a despair that is often just the other side of the most romantic and reckless hope. So the self becomes the accuser, as it so often seems only the target—the self adrift in a private universe. This, to Americans caught off base, as we all are now, can seem as frightening as the silence of those infinite spaces seemed to Pascal:

> When I consider the short duration of my life, swallowed up in the eternity before and after, the little space which I fill, and even can see, engulfed in the infinite immensity of spaces of which I am ignorant, and which know me not, I am frightened, and am astonished at being here rather than there; for there is no reason why *here* rather than *there*, why *now* rather than *then*. Who has put me here? By whose order and direction have this place and time been allotted to me?

So one writes to make a home for oneself, on paper, despite Milton's *blind Fury with the abhorréd shears, who slits the thin-spun life*. In our time history, too, can be "the blind Fury." But to write is to live it again, and in this personal myth and resurrection of our experience, to give honor to our lives.

DORIS KEARNS
Angles of Vision

The search after "the whole man" is the biographer's dream. We rummage through letters, memos, pictures, memories, diaries, and conversations in an attempt to develop our subject's character from youth to manhood to death. Yet, in the end, if we are honest with ourselves, the best we can offer is a partial rendering, a subjective portrait of the subject from a particular angle of vision shaped as much by our own biography—our attitudes, perceptions, and feelings toward the subject—as by the raw materials themselves.

Over the long years of research and writing, a biographer perceives his or her subject through inevitably shifting angles of vision. One cannot live with and worry about a subject for years without alternating feelings of anger, admiration, aggression, and affection.

I decided to write a study of Lyndon Johnson after having known him for a period of three years, the first on the White House staff, followed by two more, intermittently visiting his ranch. Initially, my feelings toward Johnson were a troubled mix of admiration and bitterness, affection and even fear. On the one hand his sheer power—and he still remains the most compelling individual I have ever met—utterly fascinated me.

One could sense his extraordinary power the moment he entered a room. There was a strange texture to the mere act of standing next to him; it seemed as if he were violating the physical space of those around him by closing in—clasping and even hugging so tightly—that people felt they had no private space left.

The other side to that fascination was fright. For the very compulsion involved in the exercise of large power, the bending of other people's wills to his, was a frightening thing to observe. His associates often worried themselves sick about entering his office, worried that he would deride their work. I heard real fear in their voices and saw it on their faces. Lyndon Johnson made you feel larger at first, because he paid so much attention to you, almost as though he were courting. And he did that with everybody, man or woman alike, until he had won them. And then, almost as if these were all passing high school romances, people's feelings suddenly became of little interest to him. You felt diminished rather than enlarged, as a result of being with him.

So despite the pull of fascination, there was always a counterbalancing need to get away, to leave, not to be owned. I kept leaving and then returning. The fascination alone would not have brought me back; it was simply too wearing. But at the time that I knew him, the last five years of his life, that peculiar power of personality was coupled with a visible and growing vulnerability. And in that stage of his life, particularly after he retired to the ranch, he shared with me a side of himself that he had not shared with many before, his longings, his private thoughts, his memories, his dreams. As I began to write, I had to learn how to distance myself, in order to describe both his ruthless power while tempering my own angry reaction to it and his vulnerability without allowing my sympathy for it to overly soften my portrait.

My original angle of vision toward Johnson was also shaped, as a biographer's always is, by the training one brings to the task. I came to my material as a political scientist. My

organizing questions revolved around leadership and government: the stuff of political science. What was it about this
man that made him so phenomenally suited for the Senate of
the 1950s and as president so mismatched to the turbulent
sixties? For me, the question was one of process, not an
evaluation of outcomes, but rather an attempt to understand
how they had happened.

Johnson preferred to manipulate men, not ideas. He
recognized, for example, that Wayne Morse wanted to seem
influential in foreign affairs. So he described in great detail a
proposed delegation to India, telling Morse that five other
senators were begging him to appoint them, making Morse
feel that if only he was on that delegation, he would be a
"figure" in foreign affairs. In fact, not one single senator had
requested the appointment since no one had yet heard of the
delegation, but when Johnson did appoint Morse one week
later, Morse was eternally grateful.

Having understood some of the sources of Johnson's
leadership, I was led to a larger question on historical context:
What made Johnson's one-to-one-bargaining, his superb
behind-the-scenes leadership, so suitable for the world of the
fifties, so faltering in the 1960s—the world of television, civil
wars in Asia, and a civil rights movement at home? The
confounding of Johnson's leadership in the sixties mirrored
the larger confusion of the American dream. Thus the title of
my book.

In retrospect, however, though the plot I perceived from
that original angle of vision worked to some extent, to a much
larger extent the real story, the human truth, was something
different, something I never fully understood as I was writing
the biography, and only came to see afterwards. The real
story was that of the gradual destruction of a giant of a man,
forced to witness the smashing of his hopes for greatness and
to live his last years removed from all real power, the only
source of energy he had ever known. Having been so
obsessive about the pursuit of power for so many years, he

had no other purpose. So in retirement he had to invent an imitation power. He was so used to staff meetings each morning with men from Capitol Hill, or with cabinet officials and White House aides, that he had to replicate those sessions back on the ranch, meeting with four or five field hands. He would call conferences to decide which fields should be plowed at what time, which cows should be given what medicine, and which tractors would be fixed when. He would force his field hands to write out assignments, so that he could check up on them in the afternoon. And at night, so accustomed was he to reading reports from vast staffs across the country that he demanded detailed reports on how many eggs had been laid at the ranch that day, how many postcards had been sold at the L.B.J. Birth House, or how many people had entered the L.B.J. Library.

Yet when all the reports were put aside, as he fell asleep and when he awakened, increasingly this lonely man would ask of his years near and at the pinnacle of power: Was it really worth it? The American people he had tried all his life to do something for, he worried, no longer appreciated him. Indeed the young for whom he had cared so much seemed to hate him. Should he have given the time instead to his wife and children; at least he could have depended on them. All of this cut him to the quick; it also cut to the very nature of the presidency, and perhaps to the pursuit of success in any field. The real question, the one I wished I had asked from the start—was whether the effort required to reach the top so distorts most personalities that they lose those human qualities that are necessary to a proportionate exercise of power.

A biographer's original angle of vision also encompasses an image of the place and the time span within which the subject's life story is played out. One would hope that the fascination most biographers feel toward the person extends equally to the place and the time. For me this was not so. For the place meant largely Texas and the times meant the first decades of the twentieth century. I was not fascinated by the first and felt I lacked perspective on the second.

Texas is a place, almost a country, in fact, that I had always seen largely in stereotype. And despite all the reading I did, all the trips I took, all the interviews I conducted, I never felt that I really came to terms with Texas. Perhaps the Irish easterner was too much inside me, both in reality and in the hidden myth of what I hoped to be, to ever allow me to comprehend Texas in other than an academic sense.

Texas did come to life, however, in the early chapters of the book, due not to me, but to Johnson's vivid recall. His memories of childhood had a physical texture. Unlike most people any easterner knows, he was living his last years in the very place he had been born—his ranch was literally one mile from his birthplace. He could walk every afternoon—and many afternoons he did—to and from these places, up the same path he had wandered as a child. Taken together these memories created a visual picture of what it was like to grow up in Texas in the first part of the century. The book lost much of this vividness when it followed Johnson away from home to college.

I believe the book became visually alive again only when Johnson came to Washington, for that city has been a deeply engaging place for me. I have found myself reacting to Washington as I did to Lyndon Johnson, with alternating awe, admiration, fascination, fear, and disdain. During my time on the White House staff, I was both drawn to and repelled by the same obsession that I was to witness in Johnson. For months I put my private life aside, saying to myself that "history" matters more and I could be helping to make it. So what if I missed a picnic or canceled a movie date—I could speak to the president of the United States. He would call me three or four times a week, ask me to wait around for a conversation with him that would usually take place between ten and eleven at night. All the other claims seemed irrelevant compared to that.

By the time I began to write the book my feelings toward Washington were as mixed as my feelings toward Johnson. I realized that if I had stayed there, given the attraction I felt for that world of power, I might have endlessly submerged my private life into a public one. Even if I had married and raised children, that never would have been central. So I felt that I had to escape that kind of obsession in myself. And that choice in that stage of my life, as Erik Erikson would say, inevitably affected the way I analyzed choices that Johnson made differently.

The dissonance between Johnson as subject and me as biographer influenced the choice of subject matter in my next book, which follows three generations of the Kennedy family. On the one hand, I did not want to turn immediately to another close study of one powerful person. I know now how fragile such an enterprise is. Despite all the memories, dreams, and conversations Lyndon Johnson shared with me—perhaps the richest material that a biographer could have—I knew I had drawn an incomplete picture. To attempt another such book about an historical figure I had never seen would have been impossible for me. So I broadened the angle of vision, choosing three generations of one family rather than one person. And yet as the vision broadened, I decided that at least the place had to be brought closer to my own geographical and intellectual home. I chose the Irish, the East, the Kennedy family.

I feel comfortable writing about the Progressive Era at the turn of the century, which will be a large part of my story. Had I been a politician, I probably would rather have been a ward boss in Boston in 1900 than one of today's media compounds of polls, hypes, and sixty-second spots. Growing up with my father, Michael Alousius Kearns, has left me naturally comfortable with both the Irish and the Catholic parts of the story. I think I have some sense of what Catholicism might have meant to the Kennedys because I know what it has meant to me.

Yet if the tale of two cultures involved in this story leans toward the Irish and against the Yankees, I suspect the Kennedys expressed the same longings that I did to be fully accepted, which meant then—and to an extent that we may not like to recognize, still means now—to become a Yankee. In fact, the Kennedys were the first family to fulfill this longing as they became the first Irish Brahmins.

Another reason for choosing the Kennedy family as my subject is that I am at a stage in my own life when family is the dominant concern. The question I bring to the Kennedy story, well aware that the biographer's real challenge is to ask the right question, not simply the one satisfactory to oneself, is how it was that Ambassador Kennedy, a man as strong and as controversial as Lyndon Johnson, could shape a family unit in which each of his children led lives certainly influenced by him, but not narrowed by his influence?

A biographer's own persona necessarily affects the biographies he writes. The best chance one has is to put the line and the style of his own life interests, fascinations, and myths in consonance with his subject's. To pull against that grain, not so much against the grain of active dislike as against the grain of nodding disinterest, would make for an uninteresting book. In other words, it is impossible to write a book about a bore without becoming boring.

The angle of vision that I have been describing thus far is the one that focuses on the subject himself. I would like to turn now to those other shifting angles of vision through which a biographer perceives and evaluates his or her materials.

Here, as elsewhere, politicians present special problems to the biographer. Though they leave behind hundreds of reams of words, we can never be exactly sure which ones are theirs and exactly what they mean. It is a politician's occupational hazard that effect comes to matter more than literal truth. So accustomed are they to speaking before audiences that most often what counts most is how the audiences react. Politicians tend to regard words as verbal and temporary, rather than written and permanent. Articulation, not analysis, is the coin of their kingdom.

This lesson was painfully driven home to me, when after listening to Johnson's proud description of his great-great-grandfather's heroic death at the Battle of San Jacinto, in Texas, I discovered that the grandfather had never even been at the battle. He was a real estate trader and had died at home in bed. But Johnson wanted an heroic relative so badly that he simply created the tale, and after retelling it dozens of times, the grandfather really came to exist in Johnson's mind.

So the powers of direct observation, as vivid as they might be, both in the White House and at the L.B.J. ranch, had to be balanced by a recognition of what Johnson was trying to convey and why. That meant checking everything, not just for its truth per se, but for the particular form in which it was expressed at a given time and how that rendition might reveal more about the continuing development of his character.

A second source of materials—interviews with associates—present a different kind of problem. The Johnson biography and Kennedy book provide contrasting examples of the problem. The tendency of President Johnson's associates is to be critical, while the tendency of President Kennedy's associates is to be admiring. This is not merely a reflection on the respective personalities of the two men. The central figures in the Johnson circle seem to be trying to break free of the intimacy and the fusion they experienced with Johnson, trying to live a life of some detachment, proving that they deserve their liberty by criticizing their former master. One first saw this passage to freedom in George Reedy's book *The Twilight of the Presidency*; one saw it later in Hubert Humphrey's memoirs. On the other hand, few of the Kennedy associates were ever as intimate with him as the Johnson associates were with Johnson. Kennedy tended to separate his social and his political friends far more sharply than Johnson did. The Kennedy men, in my judgment, are often seeking through the written word to tie bonds that they never had to the president. The admiring works become a rite of passage to a Camelot that never really existed for them.

What of *memoirs*? I had the opportunity of watching the creation of Lyndon Johnson's memoirs on what was virtually a literary assembly line. I learned how unauthentic memoirs can be, unless one understands the stage of life in which they are written, why they are being written at that time, and what audience they aim to please.

At first, Johnson expressed the hope that his book would live on in history. This quickly yielded to the immediate necessity of proving that his critics had wronged him, especially about Vietnam. Like other presidents who wrote their memoirs, he wanted to help history along toward vindicating him. But unlike them, and like his own years in the White House, he wanted it all, all at once.

Still, the memoirs might have been a vital book if they had been written in Johnson's own tongue. For his language was colorful, metaphorical, fascinating, and equal to that of many novelists. But his book was stilted, formal, bureaucratic, and tedious. He felt he had to write like a statesman; he had to speak like a "Harvard" as he would put it; he had to drain the color from his life in order to give it the appropriate dignity. I worked on two chapters of the memoirs, one on economics and one on civil rights. Initially, I simply honed his own accounts as I had heard them from him. When he read them, he turned red in the face. "Are you serious?" he asked incredulously. "Do you think you're going to have me saying these awful words in front of all those people of the United States? What will they think?" I had recounted, for example, his wonderful description of Wilbur Mills as a cautious politician, who would never let anything come out of his Ways and Means Committee unless he was certain that it would pass the House. Johnson had said, "He is always so concerned about saving his face, that someday that man will fall on his ass."

Little did he know how prescient he would have seemed

had he just left the prediction in his memoirs. But when he read that passage that he himself had said and that I had dutifully recorded, he got angry: "Don't you dare put such things in there; who am I to speak of Wilbur Mills that way? I may need him some day to get something passed in the Congress." Even in retirement, Johnson continued to be painstakingly presidential, hoping to prove that he had indeed belonged in the White House.

But before the end, as time took its toll on Johnson physically, as two heart attacks ravished him in the last years of his life, he became less guarded, almost as though, despite all his defenses, he had to tell his tale to someone in bits and pieces before it was too late. Otherwise, who would there ever be to tell the world about him?

The first heart attack was followed by a momentary euphoria. His presidential memoirs were done; there was little pressure to begin a book on the earlier years. Instead he could reminisce about them. He even seemed now to want to stay alive; he quit smoking, he drank less, he exercised regularly. For the first time since he had left the White House, he appeared, if only briefly, to be relatively contented. Not so coincidentally, his mind focused on a happier time in his career, his years as majority leader in the Senate. The control that he felt during those years now seemed in the retelling to become a metaphor to the control he was finally feeling at the ranch. There was a slower pace to his conversation now. His words went far deeper than a plastic presentation of public deeds; his candor became more than occasional. He was willing to reveal himself as both the lion and the fox.

His second heart attack turned the psychic tide. I believe that he knew in the last year and a half of his life that he was dying. And during that period he was obsessive about never being alone. It was during this time, as I described it in the book, that he would awaken me at five in the morning because he could not sleep and had to talk. His sense that he was dying unlocked his earliest memories. Over and over he recreated the scenes in which he had talked with his mother about her past. As he described her to me, she was not the same model mother he had praised two years before. The biographer finds that the past is not simply the past, but a prism through which the subject filters his own changing self-image. Before, Johnson had pictured his mother as loving, sensitive, and spiritual. Now, she was the demanding, ambitious, frustrated woman who loved him when he succeeded for her and scorned him when he failed. He decided not to go to college after high school, because in high school he had felt so pressured by her. She literally refused to talk to him for six months, to the point where he finally ran away to California to try to make it on his own. He could not; he came back in one year and acceded to all her demands, telling her that if she got him into college he would finally go. And she did get him in, though it meant staying in his room for three nights while he took the entrance exams. After that, he continued to send his essays and book reports to her, which she corrected at once and returned. The two together made a successful pair. Yet there was always the sense as Johnson described her to me, that she would love him only if he continued to succeed.

He would reveal such things in fits and starts. The next morning he would sound guilty for blaming her; he would try to take his tale back, saying: "Now, I didn't mean anything bad about my mother, she was the most wonderful, beautiful woman, and she always loved me no matter what." Soon he would offer another episode of her darker side, but this slow exorcism seemed as painful as it now was irrepressible.

Sadness welled up even more in those last years when he spoke of "the other beautiful woman" he had hoped to create—the Great Society. He had wanted her, he said, to be big and beneficent, fat and beautiful: In other words, when the federal government, through the laws he put on the books, became as fat or fatter even than the New Deal government, then he, Lyndon Johnson, would be even more loved than Franklin D. Roosevelt. Johnson lived to watch Nixon, month by month, cut his appropriations for the Great Society, and he felt, he said, that she was going to get so skinny and so ugly and so bony, that someday the American people were going to put her in a closet, refusing to look at her anymore. And alone in that closet she would die, and if she died, he said, then he too would die.

Johnson's curious metaphor became a part of his own life and eath. Two days before he died he listened to President Nixon's second inaugural and the following day to Nixon's plan for dismantling the Great Society. Then, that afternoon, this man who was so afraid of being alone that he would ask friends to sit outside his door while he napped, had a heart attack in his bed when no one else was in the house. He called the secret service but by the time they reached his room, he was dead. The fear he had felt all his life—of dying alone—had been realized.

Surfeited with such rich, dramatic material, I wish I could have waited to write the book for ten or twenty years, so that I could really understand and convey its human value. But I was a young professor at Harvard, I had to publish. I also think, if I had it to do over again, that I would have written the book backwards rather than forwards, starting with his last years on the ranch, then going back to the Senate and House years, and finally to the sources of his character in childhood: In other words, following the tale in the order he presented it to me. It might have meant a loss of analytical details, since I couldn't have built up the patterns of traits shown in his childhood and early adulthood and later in his leadership. And it might have made the narrative telling more personal and difficult. But it would have allowed me to accompany Johnson on his search for his own past, to go with him, backwards in time, as he tried, in the last years of his life, to understand who and what he was. And that journey, however difficult to describe, would have been, I believe now, a richer tale.

THEODORE
ROSENGARTEN
Stepping Over Cockleburs:
Conversations with Ned Cobb

I was a new-model missionary. In June 1971, I returned to Alabama behind the wheel of a trusty but fading Mercedes, the kind of automobile you would expect to see a European driving in the colonies. It was suited for adventure: under an iron-gray exterior its transmission was minus one forward gear and reverse, a condition that reflected not optimism on my part but the want of money to repair it. I had made certain, however, that the rearview mirrors were in working order, so that I might pick up anyone trailing me on my rounds in the countryside.

Why should I be a target for trouble? For one thing, there was no hiding the fact that I was a northerner. I switched the license plates on my car and modified my appearance with a haircut, but my voice and manners gave me away. So did that most telling aspect of my outlook on life, my apparent lack of a job. Local men my age were out working and home raising families. Here I was, a professional student, come to pry into peoples' pasts and tell them how to live. In recent years, outsiders like me had been greeted with violence in other parts of the state. Some were beaten, some shot, and some terrified when, for example, the buses they were riding were stoned and set on fire. I should say immediately that no hand ever was laid on me in Alabama that was not a loving hand. I do not belong to the ranks of legitimate heroes who gave of their flesh and emotional well-being to overthrow segregation. True, I had fantasies of adding something to their labors, but I relate to them mainly as a beneficiary. Ideas of racial justice and economic fair play had long preceded me. I have come to understand that they are as native to Alabama as hickory and sweet gum. This is not to belittle the contribution of the freedom riders, only to point out that they nurtured, rather than planted, the seeds of justice and revolt. By the year I got there, it was already evident that henceforth the state as well as the federal government would stand with the person abused by discrimination. So, the more zealous segregationists were fighting at the county and municipal levels. In one county, the chairs were removed from the public library to keep white and black children from sitting at the same tables. The children promptly sat on the floor! In another county, the public swimming pool was drained to keep the races from mingling in the water. Tallapoosa County, where I stayed, was quiet. This had not always been the case, and in my fears I imagined my work might rekindle old grudges and grate on the consciences of people who felt assured of salvation. Forty years earlier, the county was the scene of sensational violence leveled at black sharecroppers and tenant farmers who were trying to organize a union. Now I was there to interview a survivor, an old man who had shot it out with the sheriffs and served twelve years in prison. Surely his story would offend *someone*, and if the right people knew he was telling it they might want to stop him—or me.

I quickly assembled a band of protectors. LG Cobb, Ned Cobb's half-brother—because I am talking about them as people I knew and not as characters in a book, I will use their real names. Besides, the cat has long been out of the bag. Ned Cobb is the Nate Shaw of *All God's Dangers*. LG Cobb is TJ Shaw—So LG Cobb would not allow me to live below

Carrville in a derelict farmhouse exposed to the road and far from neighbors. Nor would he be happy if I found a place in Wall Street, a stretch of sand hills tucked away near the county line, where city water, paving, and medical service did not reach. So I looked elsewhere, and with the aid of my friend John Oliver, a Dadeville lawyer, I landed in a Pullman car in the hamlet of Jackson's Gap. The car stood stately in caterpillar green, adorned with the rampant kudzu vine, on a fragment of track just twenty yards from live rails of the Georgia Central Railroad. It had been renovated and presented years ago to a loyal engineer, now dead, upon his retirement from the railroad, perhaps in lieu of a gold watch. Four times a day trains streaked through the hollow and whistled halloo to the ghost of the engineer. I got to know the railroad men when they stopped to use the well, bashful yet candid men who, for buckets of ice on hot days, defended my house and passed the word along the line that I was to be looked after and left alone.

Thus insulated from external dangers, my mind fell prey to its own demons. No one seemed to feel threatened by my presence—at least not the people I thought *should* feel threatened. Did this mean that the community was ready to air out its history, to absorb a point of view it heretofore had regarded as subversive? Or was disinterest a judgment on me? Was the sight of a disheveled young man hiking around with a tape recorder in the morning and a fishing rod in the afternoon merely laughable? Did people take me for a tourist or an antique collector? I would have minded less if people saw in me an old-timey, door-to-door salesman, a purveyor of buttons and pins—I had heard of folks naming children after country peddlers.

Indeed, history had *not* lost its power to agitate; southerners never have been able to keep history at bay. In 1971, history was happening to them—to paraphrase Toynbee—right there and then. Events came so close they seemed to cut off the air to breathe. I should have considered that people were too busy living their lives to notice me anywhere near as hard as I was noticing myself. Middle-class white men listened dispassionately as I explained my work with Ned Cobb, then collared me with their own sad concern: their children were being "niggerized"—a misnomer for the effects of the invasion of youth culture into their homeland. Sons were smuggling in dope, flashy clothes, and Rolling Stones albums; daughters were sleeping with their boyfriends and boasting about it. What could I say? Meanwhile, near the mill town west of Ned Cobb's settlement, men in mixed pairs of black and white stood at crossroads, leafletting workers on their way to the mill. They were organizers for a textile union that was giving the company its toughest fight of the century. This organizing drive consumed all of the town's attention for outsiders and demonstrated to me the difference in risk for those who come to give the word and one who comes to take it.

Within the white community I was the center of my own attention, no one else's. I needed protection—not from sticks and insults but from a collapse of confidence. I was in danger of succumbing to the errantry and vain thrills of adventure. Adventure cushioned me against the test of my skills. I was an historian trained to ransack texts for gross and subtle meanings. Nowhere in that background could I call upon an iota of instruction for dealing with people. What does the historian do when his best sources are living people? Until quite recently, he generally avoided them.

But new circumstances have excited the demand for oral testimony, pushing historians and others into the field. First, the political movements of the fifties and sixties exposed us to the existence of large numbers of downtrodden people here in our own country. Those expressions of protest were not conceived the moment we happened to hear them; they had been gathering outrage and waiting. This truth knocked consensus history off the wall like Humpty Dumpty. Scholars could no longer shun the underside of the American dream—

their students would not let them. Now it is true that the biographies of dead illiterate people are almost unattainable. But the living can speak, though they may not write, and no one is more qualified than they are to tell us their stories.

Second, there is now broad agreement in the social sciences that *work* is interesting to read about. This attitude is left over from the radicals' critique and comes upon the momentary exhaustion of theory. Whether it persists or withers in the period of reaction, it has already inspired an exemplary first-person literature.

Third, the mass production of the small tape recorder turns many people into potential biographers and subjects, and we are doubtless at the gate of a flood of oral biographies. These in turn may become a major source for future written history. As Dean Rusk slyly explained at a recent annual meeting of the Oral History Association, what with thousands of papers issuing out of the offices of the Big-Decision Makers every week—signed but never seen by them—the historian can separate the wheat from the chaff only by going to the horse's mouth.

Fourth, readers seeking relief from the degraded language of politics and advertising, the language of disasters and lies, find it in the language of the heart. Truth comes to us as the seemingly unmediated word, in the confession of the grocer, or the farmer, or the policeman caught unawares by this chance to spill his life. By virtue of its publication, an oral biography is the triumph of a person over his fate. We all would like to share that triumph. But in the words of a popular song, "Everybody wants to go to heaven, but nobody wants to die." In the end, we do not find a single life that can be imitated, or one that we would imitate if we could. This letdown is one of the chief pleasures of reading biography, the satisfaction that you are not the other person.

In the marketplace for oral history, the field worker offers up his spoken treasures as a boldfaced commodity. Here he reverts to his own social class. You would think he would relish this chance to be himself after long months of suspending his normal behavior. But it is tough to fall back into the old groove. You come home bodily, but the integrity of the ideas you have encountered nags at your mind. What began as a kind of innocent subterfuge designed to get people to talk to you or merely to tolerate you ends as a reproach against your previous outlook. I do not know a way around this dilemma, especially for white field workers who approach colored people. (This is a twist on the familiar observation that nonwhites are always "putting on" whites.)

The field worker's artifice consists of a sudden respect for tradition and an earnestness verging on sainthood. Take me, for example: at home I had no use for religion, I harangued against the nuclear family, I scoffed at celebrating personal and public anniversaries. But in the field I was an ardent supporter of traditional elements against the attacks of modernism. I was ready to agree with LG Cobb that atheism is a symptom of mental illness. I did not feel that I was being false—conscience tells me I did not give in to wanting to be liked. But neither was I a true convert to the norms I was newly defending. In effect, I had faith without belief.

Not all of my values were so ephemeral. I believed that the country needed a revolution—I still believe it—and I was not shy about saying so. But what sounded like politics to me was religion to the Cobbs. Politics, where I came from, took in religion. But to them, religion had no difficulty taking in politics. Try as I would to say something new, they already had a way of expressing it. The breadth of their perspective should have pleased me because it meant we had a larger meeting ground than I had ever expected; but instead it frustrated me, it took away the analytical superiority that every field worker thinks he holds in reserve whenever his ignorance of the natural and social worlds threatens to betray him.

The field worker is a serious person. He appears most resolute when the purpose of his labors has escaped him entirely. The only humor he is likely to add to a situation comes in the form of a blunder. My first evening in Alabama I committed a telling little error, one of the type that occurs unavoidably the moment a field worker steps in the field. It was the kind of thing that is good for a laugh, and had I not dreaded being laughed at, I could have appreciated both the comedy and its ingratiating effect on my hosts. They made a little story out of it and broadcasted it in the family. It preceded me from home to home, assured me of a friendly welcome, and facilitated my work as no other introduction could have done.

I drove up to LG's place and found no one at home. It was suppertime—I had a knack for showing up just as people were sitting down to eat—and his car and truck were in the yard. Going to look for him at the vegetable garden, I caught sight of four people slow-stepping along freshly plowed rows about eighty yards diagonally across the field from me. Two women were leading two men, the women bending in curtsies every few feet, the men poking harmoniously at the ground with walking sticks. They appeared not to move a muscle of their own; their figures were disassembled and put together again in new positions by the playful last light. LG and his crowd were planting sweet potatoes. I took off running across the field with a notebook in one hand and my tape recorder flapping against my side. Why hadn't I left this baggage at my car? I certainly had no intention of using it out there. Yet with sword and buckler I ran—not far, however, until I stopped short. With each running step I was mashing down the green shoots of some nameless plant. It was hard to see in the dark, but that was no excuse. A cow would have more sense. LG, his wife Glennie—Winnie, in the book—and their helpers stopped what they were doing to watch me approach. I waved and the men waved back. But I could not look up as I picked my way to them, I had to look at the ground. Here a skip, there a leap—the little green devils popped up everywhere to trip me! At last I reached them by a broken route. We shook hands, embraced, I was introduced to Glennie's son and daughter-in-law, and they went on with their task. The women walked ahead putting down potato slips every two feet in adjoining rows. The men followed nudging the root ends into the earth with their sticks. Setting out potato slips was easygoing, sociable work. I tagged along, taking in the strange smells and sights. I felt heavy-footed, but giddy, cured of my first anxiety: Would they welcome me? After a minute, no more, LG asked me what I was doing, hopping out there like that. I said I was avoiding stepping on the plants. What plants are those, he asked. Cotton or corn, I guessed. No, the field had not been planted yet. I was stepping over cockleburs, the spiny nemesis of cultivated fields. Oh, they had a big laugh then, stepping over weeds the boy is!

Happily for my work, if not for my state of mind, I had put myself on the spot. I know now that I am fortunate among field workers for having been found out so soon. The Cobbs took an interest in my education from the start, not for any material reward—there was no prospect of any—but because my search had a religious quality they could not resist. They were stuck with me, knowing that I would keep coming back to interrupt their work and their rest with perpetual questions. If only I would be satisfied with information, the chore would have an end. But I wanted to learn a way of thinking, something more private than information, more revealing. I was seeking their reflections, the stories they told themselves about themselves. The radical in me preached about the future, but the would-be disciple asked about the past—to the obvious neglect of the present. In the absence of my people I needed to be fed and cared for, and they were glad to do it. They helped me as Christians, and beyond that by the creative effort of enclosing me in the family.

This raises the question of the place of *love* in social science inquiry. The word causes a great deal of embarrassment in the profession. We talk about cooperation and gratitude when we mean something more profound. But without an accurate description of the feelings that pass between the inquirer and his subject, the utility of the interview or data that emerges from that relationship is seriously impaired. Perhaps we divest our motivations of love because we fear an attack on our objectivity. Yet, no claim of objectivity survives the generation in which it is made. Before the ink has dried, the writer's stake in his work begins to show through, like the watermark of a fine paper. It may be that the writer had a private interest of which he was aware all along. Or it may have nothing to do with individual ambition, but with the compulsions of social class enacted unconsciously in every relationship. To talk of objectivity, then, is to talk of concealment.

I do not say that it behooves the field worker to fall in love with his subjects. Romantic or rapturous involvement diverts him from his work and sows the seeds of the injury his subjects are bound to feel when he makes their secrets public. Given the risks, he is probably better off to leave love alone, to tread a more lighthearted path. But if it happens—what I am calling love—it should not be smoothed over in the field worker's acknowledgments.

There was one special reason why Ned Cobb's family agreed to busy itself with me, apart from the feelings between us. My work with Ned revived his will to live. The doctor had given him a prescription of small brown pills for a heart condition, but he refused to take them and would put them out in the bird feeder. At eighty-five years old, his appetite had left him: a tablespoon of peanut butter, a small piece of cornbread, and several cups of coffee a day were all he was eating. He would not eat meat or vegetables—he remembered that his father had died with a mouthful of greens. Consequently, he was losing weight. He still had the energy to keep a small garden and a hog, and the concentration to make baskets—working white oak, he called it. But he no longer had the strength to get out in the woods, cut down a tree, and carry it home. Walking the roads was hazardous now that his sight and hearing were failing and, of course, he did not drive. He was confined more or less to idle hours in one place. Although he was a thoughtful man, it did not suit him to sit still and meditate. Inactivity depressed him; he could not stand the thought of his time lying fallow. In short, he was suffering through the most drastic change of his life. He had always been a talkative man and now talking had become his only means of engaging attention. But his moodiness, self-concern, and tendency to repeat himself chased away visitors and deepened his isolation.

Then I came along with the expressed intent of listening to what he had to say. Immediately, he perked up, as old people often do when they feel the devotion of younger ones. I had kept my promise, given four months before, to return and record his life story. Three mornings a week for three months we would sit and talk on the veranda of his toolshed or inside the shed when it rained. There, amid heaps of guano sacks, moldy harnesses, broken tools, and bottomless chairs we had our most memorable conversations. We did not miss a day, nor did I once have to urge him out of his house to begin work. He would wake up earlier than usual to get his little jobs out of the way and to clear a place for us to sit. When I showed up, at last, he would greet me with a comment about how late into the morning it was, or how he came into this world "to work out, not rust out," or how he hoped I had installed "longliving" batteries in the tape recorder this time. Many a morning he wore me out. At the end of three hours he was just getting cranked up, but my tank was empty. He would refuse to stop talking when the tape recorder ran down, as if to demonstrate his vitality over the machine and the folly of trying to cramp the shape and flow of a life, *his* life, into a little black box. On my lucky days, his wife Sarah— Josie, in the book—would rescue me with the call to come to dinner. Reluctant and mute he would show me to the washstand, then escort me to the table. I told him, politely, that I would not eat alone—Sarah, her granddaughter, and her great-grandchildren would already have eaten—and he was obliged to eat with me. In this way we took a dozen meals together, and though he never attacked his food with much interest, he would eat enough to keep me eating.

Sometime in July, Ned's sister-in-law died in Birmingham and her body was brought home for burial. After the funeral, Ned's sons "caucused" to take up the matter of the young white man from the North who, in full view of the settlement, was interrogating their father. I learned about this meeting several years later. The upshot of it was, they resolved not to interfere in our business and even to assist it if they could. This decision might appear to have been easy to reach, seeing how talking strengthened Ned. After all, what are the suspicions and jealousies of neighbors next to the health of a father! But when fathers talk about their lives, they must talk about their children; and what is social history to the outside reader is really Papa talking about family affairs. No one doubted Ned's loyalty, but no one had much faith in his discretion, either. I was ignorant at the time of the children's courage in allowing our work to flourish; unaware, too, that I was encouraging the very impetuousness in Ned that could lead to their betrayal.

Ned Cobb had no hesitation. He was racing against time to give his last confession. From me he wanted the affirmation he felt he had never gotten from his children—that he had always tried to do the right thing. Moreover, he was speaking to a higher judge. By offering up his good works as proof of his intentions, he pinned his salvation on God's justice, not mercy. If he erred on the side of righteousness, he gambled that this last deed would win him forgiveness. The lies he exposed were monumental compared to the lies he concealed. He wanted his testimony to oppose the stories told about people like him in newspapers, court records, congressional reports, merchants' ledgers, and school books. He did not know—to paraphrase Marcel Griaule's estimation of the unforgettable Ogotemmeli—that he was contributing mightily to revolutionizing society's ideas about the mentality of black people.

Our collaboration was the meeting of a hero of the past with a young man who needed to make something of himself; of a person of extraordinary verbal skills with one poorly trained to listen but who knew how to operate a tape recorder. I never considered myself an oral historian, nor the field I was working in oral history. I have always felt that the term is misleading, condescending, and plain bad speech. Oral history stresses the means, not the end, and it does a poor job at that. The technique involved is more *aural* than oral, though "aural history" won't do, either. When you think of social history or political history you have a pretty good notion that you are dealing with recognizable people and institutions; but oral history tells you nothing of the historian's special area of concern, which can be as varied as that of the historian who works from written artifacts. Oral history suggests a fad, like 3-D movies or see-through clothing. But in fact it has been around a very long time. Oral history is the incarnation of the ancestor of all written histories—the epic poem. Of course, not all oral histories are epics, and some epics are epic bores.

I used a tape recorder in my work because my subject demanded it. Some people start with technical expertise, then go looking for a subject, but that was not the case with me. Inevitably, my work was full of mistakes that might have been avoided had I been taught to interview. But I was taught to distrust the spoken word, especially if the speaker were still alive. Are we to believe that the dead tell the truth and the living tell lies? This morbid attitude cripples the study of the recent past and discourages contact with humanity, or with that great part of humanity that has neither the time nor the learning to write things down.

But the view of the tape recorder as a gimmick and as a conspirator in the devaluation of language is not a frivolous one. Oral history—to bow to popular usage—may be an unwitting tool in the extinction of the oral tale. Frequently it is the stopping place of the tale; recording and transcribing remove it from the orbit of the teller, putting an end to his creative intervention. You could argue that by the time the tales are recorded they no longer produce the teller's desired effects; that the social and economic worlds of the tales are defunct and the lessons we draw from them are worthless in modern times. As late as 1950, for example, a cotton farmer in Alabama needed to know how to break and drive a mule; soon afterwards, mules disappeared and the farmer who could not work a tractor had to withdraw from the field. Tales about mules lost their utility, except as amusements. The tape recorder, coming on the heels of radio, television, motion pictures, and other mechanical voices of culture that have invaded the exotic society and blunted the urge to hear a story, saves these cheapened scraps of wisdom from oblivion.

But it can be said of oral tales in writing, as of organic objects preserved by glaciers, that the soul has fled. Not that the tales lose their capacity to entertain or to teach, or that the personality of the teller fails to shine through; but the fixity of the form shifts to the reader the power to vary the meanings of the tales. It is true that the tape recorder carries the tales to an audience the size and variety of which the teller never dreamed. Well, yes; but the teller in his native setting does not intend the same tale, told exactly the same way, for every listener. I heard Ned Cobb tell a particular story five or six times to different people. He would vary a mood, add or omit a detail, shift himself from foreground to background, to produce the effect he wanted. He had one version for his family, one for the neighbors, one for traveling salesmen, and one for me—and they were all the same story, each told with the personality of the listener in mind.

Take the story of Ned's shootout with the deputy sheriffs. In the version for outsiders, he happens to be visiting his brother-in-law one morning when he hears a ruckus across the road at Cliff James's (Virgil Jones's) place, and he goes to investigate; in the general version for family and friends, he is determined to take his stand the morning of the trouble, though the gunplay catches him by surprise; and in the version told to like-minded allies, he packs a .32 Smith and Wesson and expects to have to use it. What you hear depends on how much he trusts you. Yet no version is false, once you know all the versions. Each reveals one of the hats he wore—bystander, soldier, plotter. Each is a step on the way to the next, contained in but not contradicted by his other positions. Privately, no one version satisfied him. He spent hours upon hours listening to himself on tape, all the while scolding the voice for leaving out some detail or including the wrong ones, or misrepresenting some attitude or feeling. Talking to me he unquestionably favored his more heroic positions, but at the cost of a certain peace of mind. Among his everyday contacts he could count on having opportunities to tell his tale a little differently, to bring out the innocent or un-self-conscious self lurking in the other tellings.

Take the story about doping a hog with his urine and turning it into a pet. I heard him tell it one morning to his "great-grands," his wife's great-grandsons, who were pestering his hog some way; he left out the urine part and made it a lecture on the affection a man should feel for his beasts. Telling the same story to a band of men who walked out of the woods one day hunting a loose hog, Ned emphasized how he had fooled *his* hog, and what a trifling mind a hog has compared to man. Sitting and listening to Ned was as good a way as any to hunt the hog, for the hog was sure to circle back to its trough in time for its next meal. The tale was reassuring insofar as it forecast the hog's return. But it disturbed the listeners, too, because the moral of it was: Don't waste your time hunting a hog that's bound to come home on its own.

Two shocks—the first like the sudden throwing of a railroad switch, the second like a derailment—shaped the course of my work. The first came at the beginning. After three hours of talking with Ned I had not asked him a single question from the more than one hundred pages of questions I had on my lap. I had spent the last eight months devising the questions from my readings on cotton culture, Alabama state history, the black family, the black church, etc., any material that could help me anticipate the language Ned would use to talk about his life. *He* had spent much of the past forty years— from the time he went off to prison—sorting out his experiences and putting them into a life history. He divided his life into four periods that corresponded conceptually to what I knew as "life stages": from birth through reaching his majority; from marriage through the formation of his family and the day he took his stand; prison; and the confounding years of old age. Actually, there was a fifth period. I became aware of it the day he told me about a swap he had made involving a horse, some dogs, and a shotgun. I asked him exactly when that was, and he said, "Oh, that happened when I was an old man." He stopped smiling and sank into alarm, as if by realizing he was outliving old age he was bringing bad luck on himself. "If I was an old man then," his countenance asked, "what am I now?"

He had it all on the tip of his tongue, "the diagrounds" and "the marrow." All I would have to do is sit still and listen and he would tell it. This meant setting aside my questions, all of which I considered crucial. They were the foundation of my composure, and what they lacked in spontaneity they made up in astuteness—or so I thought. I was glad to give up some of the day-to-day responsibility for carrying us forward, but I was distressed at having to surrender my will. When it came to transcribing and editing our talks I would recoup my power, but I did not know that at the time. I was reeling from a collision with this foreign intelligence, and I had to adapt in a hurry.

Ned began by talking about his father. It was more like wrestling, the way he was agitated. I turned to the page in my notebook entitled "Family Relations," but the questions seemed flat, artificial, and hopeless. As prompters they made good roadblocks. Pretty soon I abandoned them and began to listen to what *he* was saying. I heard Isaac rail against Abraham, the son against the father who, in the ancient heretical tradition, was ready to sacrifice the boy as much out of recklessness as for gain. His father did not know how to provide for his wives, his children, or himself. He hastened the death of Ned's mother by overworking her; he denied Ned, the eldest son, the chance to go to school and put him behind a plow before he was big enough to do the job. While his family worked he was out gratifying his passions—chiefly hunting and carousing with outside women. He toted a gun against imagined enemies but when it was time to stand up to the white men who periodically came to dispossess him, he did not have a word or deed to offer. Ned softened the portrait by adding that his father had been brutalized by slavery and carried within him "slavery ways"; that there was nothing wrong, per se, in pursuing pleasure, though the old man went overboard; that the white man was too strong to oppose in his father's day; that his father had to conceal his knowledge of the world or incur the wrath of those who controlled the purse strings and the police.

As he laid out his life in the course of the summer, Ned discovered a good deal of his father in himself. There were fundamental differences between them, of course. Ned was a great provider, a fighter, an enterprising and sober man. Everyone who knew him verified these qualities. Outwardly, the contrast between Browne Cobb (Hayes Shaw) and Ned Cobb could not be more pronounced. Inside, the son like the father was a *hard* man—loving, but hard. Sometimes his meanness flew off in the wrong directions, as when he disciplined his boys—which he does not tell us about—or simply blamed them for things that were not their fault, or failed to give them credit for what they achieved on their own. The stories of his adult years are full of fatherly disrespect—the very "flaw" he condemned in his father. Of his quick temper and stubbornness he would say, "I was *natured* that way." At first it was an embarrassing admission; then he took pride in that, too, because he saw that his distinction lay in his heredity.

He did not consider what he may have inherited from his mother, only from his father. He grew up in a patriarchy and he believed that fathers should attend to sons and mothers to daughters—at least until the daughters reach courting age. Ned credited his father with instilling in him the power to "interpretate" events and to size up a white man. Browne Cobb, despite his localized sphere of interests, had an eye to the larger world. Many times Ned would unravel a situation with one of his father's aphorisms, a bit of poetic advice culled from a long life of ducking punches. It made Ned happy to think that his father was a man who used his mind, and that he had picked up the habit.

But his inheritance included the *hardness*. In him flowed the "isms" or habits of slavery that had worked their way into his father like worms into fruit. Ned had cut out the most debilitating of these habits, but the others, he feared, would pass on to his sons. He detected in them the "weak point" he so hated in his father—the neglect to ever tell *him* that he had done the right thing. How was a father to think well of himself without the validation of his sons? Come judgment day, who would intercede for him if not them? But to tell the truth, Ned's sons—and daughters—recognized him to the world for his good works and protected his reputation against outside criticism. If they failed to acknowledge to his face the stand that he took in Cliff James's yard, it was not because they opposed his ideals or lacked his courage. Rather, they believed he had miscalculated his support the morning of the shootout. They, not he, bore the brunt of hardships when he was away in prison. *They* lost a father; *they* watched as the task of leading a large family through perilous times took a fatal toll on their mother. When Ned returned he tried to take up the reins to his family and his farm; but his children were grown and would not be bossed about things they had mastered in his absence, and the farm was prospering in the hands of his older sons. All of this sensitive history was debated in the universal family way: with avoidance, petty quarrels, sulking, shouting matches, and silence. Ned clung to his old thoughts but the day had changed. Time had dealt him a blow that his enemies could never muster. A great economic depression had been overcome, a world war had been fought, the tractor had been introduced to southern agriculture. Where in all of this did he belong? His struggle to recover his old authority over house and field was sure to lose. He fell into talking about the man he once was; the older he got the more clearly he recalled his boyhood days.

At some point in his recollecting he must have begun to see that one experience after another yielded the same lesson: figure out the enemy, stand up with a clear conscience, and you can win! Not by a throw of the dice did he find himself standing up for justice in Cliff James's yard that morning. He was there because his whole life led him there; everything before had been merely preparation. The shootout put all of his early skirmishes into perspective. It was the grandest piece of a design, a fate, sealed in his character. It was also the end of his epoch, the years of his climb. He belonged back then.

One of those fortunate turns in the histories of oppressed peoples enabled Ned to see himself in a new light and to shed the despondency of isolation. The Civil Rights movement carried his spirit forward in time: it was *of* him, just as he had been *of* it. He perceived himself as part of the advance guard and as an agent of prophecy. When I met him in 1968 he told me his grandmother had told him that white people had come from the North after "the surrender" to help black people secure their freedom, but they had left the job undone and someday would return to complete it. Ned met them in the thirties when they came in the form of the

Sharecroppers Union. "The organization," as he called it, "was workin to bring us out of the bad places where we stood at that time and been standin since the colored people has remembrance," but it, too, was stopped short of the goal. In the fifties and sixties they came again, a shock and a "wonderment" to many, but "expectable" to Ned.

To his way of thinking, social and economic salvation would bring about a change in human personality. The movement in all of its eruptions meant "a turnabout on the southern man, white and colored." This means first of all the redistribution of power, the bottom rail rising and the top rail falling. But the predicate, "man, white and colored," implies a psychological shift as well. Whites will stop feeling superior, and blacks will stop acting inferior—in the sense of acting badly to themselves. Then the "isms" of the past, embodied in law, custom, and personal conduct, will be rooted out at last. By the measure of one lifetime the process seems interminable. Even across three lifetimes the velocity of change would frustrate a snail. But if a person cannot hope to savor the ultimate victory, he can improve himself by taking part in the movement of his day. Such participation does not have to be voluntary or self-conscious. Everyone may benefit from victories won by a few—victories over disease, over manual labor, over economic exploitation. The standards people live up to become a force against backsliding. Ned's father could never have been reenslaved, and now his children would never accept segregation. Ned, standing between the two generations, separating and linking them, occupied all of the possible positions in the social and family struggles. Factually, he was the son of his father and the father of his children. But in jousting with his father he performed the part of his own sons against himself, and their grievances unfolded. By projecting his father's points onto them, he suggested a response Browne Cobb might have made to Ned's complaints about him.

The morning this cathartic drama opened, I was

fumbling with my papers in my lap and asking myself: How does this fit into history? Will my teachers think I am crazy? I meant: Is life history *history*? If Thoreau is right, and all anyone has to report is a human experience, then isn't this a breakthrough, because it is so alarmingly human? These were not bad questions, but it was the wrong time to be asking them.

Back at the railroad car, I played over the morning's tape to check out the machine and to hear how I came across. I was astonished at how little of Ned's talk had reached my inner ear. The problem was, I had set out to question, not to listen. My mind was full of chatter and thoughts about my questions. I had not listened at all. I had allowed my machine to do the listening for me, when I should have done it for myself. Let the machine record, and you listen! Afterwards there will be time to listen to the recording with an adversarial ear. This listening is really a kind of deliberation, and it is different from the listening appropriate to the performance of a tale.

You need to listen both ways. Listening is the key, pure listening and deliberate listening. They do not overlap. If you are making mental notes you cannot be emptying your mind of thought. Whenever I was stymied, I found it incredibly relaxing to listen to our talks with no conscious thinking, neither seeking nor judging. Going back to pure listening had the effect of sharpening my *sense* of Ned. That sense was *in the listening*, the way that meaning belongs to a process and not to an end. In putting together Ned's autobiography, I tried to choose those tales and versions of tales that most closely conformed to this sense—or essence—of him.

I got into a pattern of listening deliberately to our tapes the evenings of the days we recorded. In these hours I planned questions to ask at the start of our next session—a prerogative I had to fight for. I listened for gaps in the stories, and I would ask Ned to fill in wherever I thought a *reader* would need it. I took my ignorance as the standard, especially in regard to the natural world. Out of one such request for elaboration came the lyrical passages on the boll weevil.

I listened for allusions to people or incidents I wanted to hear more about. We could not take all roads, but I wanted to minimize my regrets for the roads not taken. My interest in a character might have led Ned to give him more weight in his narrative than he had in life. Beaufort Jackson—Lemuel Tucker, in the book—comes to mind, a white landlord who tried to sell him the shoes off his feet and died broke in a boarding house in town.

I listened for extraordinary events dispassionately told, such as the burning down of the prison barns; and mundane events told with great emotion, such as taking a ride on a milk truck. These reports clarified the distance between us that would never be overcome. What was exceptional to one of us might be ordinary to the other because of the discrepancy in our experiences. I did not find a way to render Ned's inflection in prose. Nothing I asked elicited a satisfactory substitute in words for these lost facts of feeling.

I listened also for inconsistencies. For some reason I thought these were very important, and that the way to deal with them was to challenge Ned to justify the facts. Does it matter that a horse is brown in one story and gray in another? Or that Ned drove his '28 Ford to town in 1926? It matters, but more for what it tells us about the teller's method than his memory. When I pointed out these inconsistencies, Ned grew indignant. They were not questions of remembrance, he assured me. And he would say no more. His silence was his way of telling me I was impinging on his right to choose the elements of his stories. We were collaborators, true, but we each had discrete functions and privileges. I chose the day, the hour, and the duration of our sessions; I would make the cruel choice of closing down the talks; I would choose where to take our "report" and what to do with it, how to edit it, who to publish it. But the choice of words was his.

No book worth the paper it is printed on will please everyone. I was not disheartened, therefore, when *All God's*

Dangers had its immediate detractors. They argued that a black man never tells a white man the truth; that the writer molded the teller's words to fit a flagrant bias; that the protagonist is not typical, and therefore his narrative is esoteric; that I was guilty of "sharecropping" off a helpless black man. More friendly commentaries showed how I had misheard words and phrases. For example, I wrote "dew rock" when Ned said, or should have meant to say, Duroc, the hardy American red hog. Except for the strange insinuation that my ignorance of farming disqualified me from learning about it, I was grateful for the corrections. I was totally unprepared, however, for the judgment that came from a very different quarter, from people I had wanted most to please—Ned Cobb's children.

There are nine children: five who live in cities outside of Alabama and four who never left, three of whom live within a mile of Ned's last home. The children did not know me only, or mainly, as the person who had questioned their father; and I did not know them only as Ned Cobb's children. They were, in the words of one of the sons, their "own self-ladies and own self-men." My awareness of this was a condition of our friendship. I had interviewed most of them in their homes with the tentative aim of producing a family history. When I visited I often stayed over—as a guest, a courier among brothers and sisters, and—I do not think it farfetched to say— a loved one. Like any nine individuals, the children of Ned Cobb have their own minds about things; and like any children of a single family they have intrinsically more to agree or to disagree about than strangers do. They did not all respond the same way to their father's autobiography. Yet they did not exactly disagree, either. I am talking about gut feelings, first feelings, what transpired when a two-pound book as thick as a standard Bible, with a picture of their father as a young man on the cover, arrived out of the blue, brimming with his old man's voice, his old man's stories, his old man's philosophies and complaints. I delivered copies first to the two children in Alabama who had nourished me and waited on me since I had been coming south. I hung around Tallapoosa County to give them a chance to read it, or to read their part in it, what their father had said about them. When I went back to see them they told me straight out: they were deeply offended. Ned had told too much and I lacked the sensitivity to leave it out. His obsession to talk had betrayed them, and I had published the betrayal! In those terrible moments I lost my youth and godliness. Oh, to be stepping over cockleburs again! My world caved in. I was never so shocked in my life.

Wilbur Cobb—Vernon, to readers—is the hero of the second half of the book. It was he who, along with his mother, held the family together when Ned was off in prison. Sturdy and gentle as the fiber of cotton, he is the last of the Cobbs still farming. Ned had told me of a quarrel they'd had about a year after Ned married Sarah, three years or so after the death of his first wife, Viola (Hannah). The story is curiously absent of motive, like the melodrama of a still-life painting. They were driving home from a funeral in Wilbur's truck, Ned, Wilbur, and Wilbur's wife, "just talking like people would talk . . . and it come like a shot—." According to Ned, Wilbur raised up and hollered, "'You just ain't got no sense!'" This was followed by brooding silence, an exchange of threats, and other "bad words." Nothing much came of it except that for one week they kept their distance and did not talk.

Why would Wilbur tell his father he had no sense? Between strangers the remark would be gratuitous. But between a son and a father it may be the judgment of a lifetime. Then again, it may not. We do not know from the text. Ned suggests that Wilbur had been drinking—but the accusation is absurd. He does not drink. Furthermore, there is no room in the story for him to have slipped off to drink. Something is missing here.

Wilbur was insulted by the story. His father had

disclosed the kind of family business that ought not to travel through the settlement. On top of that was the personal hurt. How could Wilbur defend himself against cold print? Who would know what Ned had left out? It would compound my wrongdoing to tell that here, but I learned enough to know that I owed Wilbur an apology. I tried to assure him that Ned's story was not plausible; no one would believe it. But I must have believed it, he said, because I had it printed. No, I had not considered whether it was complete or true; those were not my criteria. The story was important to me because it humanized Ned. It cleansed him of purity when he thought he was cleansing himself of sin. I was ashamed for hurting Wilbur, I wished he could feel differently—but I still thought the story belonged in the book. What good is an apology if you would do the same thing over again if you had the chance? There was no way out of feeling bad.

Driving north, I delivered books to two of Ned's daughters in Chattanooga, to a son in Middletown, Ohio, to a son in Philadelphia, and to a daughter in Brooklyn. Had *All God's Dangers* been the trial for them that it was for their siblings in Alabama, I would be restoring antique automobiles or catching crabs for my living today. But the children in the North were able, by and large, to take the family business with the social history, the "ugliness" with the "prettiness," because, as one of the daughters put it, "the good is so overwhelming." Yes, most of it is true, what he said; there was more truth than you expect to find in a book. But don't think this was all Ned Cobb had been or done! His daughters recalled times he had struck out against people he shouldn't have; but a certain worldliness acquired in the years away from home made them see something positive even in these assertions. It troubled them to find so little in the book about their mother. Ned had diminished her role, they decided, not to take credit for something of *hers*, but out of common masculine forgetfulness. It had troubled Ned, too, he confessed in the book, that he had recognized his wife too late and too little. Ned repeatedly confessed to more than he consciously knew—that, for example, if he did not worship his mules he certainly adored them; that when it came to quarreling in his house he held up his end rather than make peace. His autobiography was not the portrait of a hypothetical man, but the breath of their precious, imperfect father about whom they could say, "We know you." They could rejoice in his triumph because it was not a triumph over them, but with them and for them. Ned believed that his physical accomplishments were his bestowal to future generations. But they knew that his gift was his *mental being*, the activity and reach of his mind.

One year later—two years after Ned Cobb's death—I visited my friends in Alabama to learn the impact of the book. I wanted to see if time had soothed or exacerbated first feelings, and to test my welcome. The drive from Montgomery to Tallapoosa County seemed shorter, perhaps because the city was spreading so fast the distance between them was actually closing. How many of the old country houses had disappeared since I'd first driven through seven years earlier! In place of the single-pen, dogtrot, and saddlebag farm houses rose the bungalows, brick ranches and mobile homes of people who worked *off* the land. The old way of life and the old-timey people were finished. Ned was gone—he did not live to see his book. His brothers LG and Paul (Peter) had died suddenly within six months of Ned. Between the harvesting of one crop and the planting of another, the last of the nineteenth-century-born Cobbs had left this world. LG died not long after moving into the house he'd built on his own land. He'd built it from a plan he kept in his head, using lumber he had salvaged from two churches. You could tie your tie in the luster of the hard-pine floor. LG had been a cotton farmer his whole life, some years working in the mill by day and on his farm in the evening. Once he had dreams of playing professional baseball—he was the size of Frank Howard—and he drove to Birmingham to try out with the Birmingham Black Barons of the Negro Baseball League. But the Barons were out of town, the stadium was locked shut, and LG returned to his farm to stay. Paul was half LG's size, a good eight inches under Ned. He lived most of his life within three miles of where he was born, on Saugahatchee (Sitimachas) Creek. He had quit farming when I met him and was living with his wife Bessie in a very old house that he got in return for minding the landowner's cows. Paul had been "quiet-lifed," as Ned called it. He decided as a young man that if he didn't have a lot of possessions he couldn't be hurt by losing them. Paul was a subsistence farmer by choice, and he prospered without money. He was revered in his settlement for his knowledge and graciousness. I've seen white men squat while *he* sat, talking under his pecan trees.

I stopped first to see Roberta (Rachel), Ned's oldest daughter. She had recently retired from a small broom factory nearby, and was devoting her energies to her house and garden. In spring her yard would be popping with tulips and gladiolas. From knowing her sons, eating her cooking, and observing her devotion to her flowers, I had concluded that if I hadn't had a mother of my own, she was someone I would want for the job. But it was not the best of times between us. She had been upset by the book, and angry with me, for unmasking old troubles. We did not get far talking about the book. To Roberta, it was a piece of bad luck slowly receding into the past; like the tree of knowledge there was no real knowledge to it, only sadness and judgment. To me, it was a history of cotton farming in all of its relations, seized upon and epitomized by a man who grew the cotton—and *that* was sacred. There was no bridging our opinions that day.

I wanted something impossible: for Roberta to regard the book from the historical point of view. But to all of Ned Cobb's children, their father can represent only himself. He could do no more than that in life; and now, living on in remembrance, he is more the father and less the man of all the other roles he played before. In the historical view, Ned will one day be typical—but not yet, not yet! The more that is learned about his age the more he will appear to speak its language and think its thoughts, as a conformist and a dissenter. There is sufficient evidence in his narrative and in the testimony of those who knew him to call his genius unique. But I am convinced that the life stories of his contemporaries would reveal equally valiant responses to the same social forces. Ned would not fall then in our estimation any more than would the hero of a battle when it is learned that there had been other heroes as well. He was the first to convey to the book-taught world the whole life of an unlettered tenant farmer. His autobiography became an occasion to cut through the official memory of written history with the keenness of a drawknife and the immediacy of "a butterbean bursting in the sun."

BARBARA W. TUCHMAN
Biography as a Prism of History

In so far as I have used biography in my work, it has been less for the sake of the individual subject than as a vehicle for exhibiting an age, as in the case of Coucy in *A Distant Mirror*; or a country and its state of mind, as in the case of Speaker Reed and Richard Strauss in *The Proud Tower*; or an historic situation, as in the case of *Stilwell and the American Experience in China*. You might say that this somewhat roundabout approach does not qualify me for the title of biographer and you would be right. I do not think of myself as a biographer; biography is just a form I have used once or twice to encapsulate history.

I believe it to be a valid method for a number of reasons, not the least of which is that it has distinguished precedents. The National Portrait Gallery uses portraiture to exhibit history. Plutarch, the father of biography, used it for moral examples: to display the reward of duty performed, the traps of ambition, the fall of arrogance. His biographical facts and anecdotes, artistically arranged in *Parallel Lives*, were designed to delight and edify the reader while at the same time inculcating ethical principles. Every creative artist—among whom I include Plutarch and, if it is not too pretentious, myself—has the same two objects: to express his own vision and to communicate it to the reader, viewer, listener, or other consumer. (I should add that as regards the practice of history and biography, "creative" does not mean, as some think, to invent; it means to give the product artistic shape.)

A writer will normally wish to communicate in such a way as to please and interest, if not necessarily edify, the reader. I do not think of edifying because in our epoch we tend to shy away from moral overtones, and yet I suppose I believe, if you were to pin me down, that esthetic pleasure in good writing or in any of the arts, and increased knowledge of human conduct, that is to say of history, both have the power to edify.

As a prism of history, biography attracts and holds the reader's interest in the larger subject. People are interested in other people, in the fortunes of the individual. If I seem to stress the reader's interest rather more than the pure urge of the writer, it is because, for me, the reader is the essential other half of the writer. Between them is an indissoluble connection. If it takes two to make love or war or tennis, it likewise takes two to complete the function of the written word. I never feel my writing is born or has an independent existence until it is read. It is like a cake whose only raison d'être is to be eaten. Ergo, first catch your reader.

Secondly, biography is useful because it encompasses the universal in the particular. It is a focus that allows both the writer to narrow his field to manageable dimensions and the reader to more easily comprehend the subject. Given too wide a scope, the central theme wanders, becomes diffuse, and loses shape. The artist, as Robert Frost once said, needs only a sample. One does not try for the whole but for what is truthfully *representative*.

Coucy, as I began to take notice of him in my early research on the fourteenth century, offered more and more facets of the needed prism. From the time his mother died in the Black Death to his own marvelously appropriate death in the culminating fiasco of knighthood that closed the century, his life was as if designed for the historian. He suppressed the peasant revolt called the Jacquerie; he married the king of England's eldest daughter, acquiring a double allegiance of great historical interest; he freed his serfs in return for due payment (in a charter that survives); he campaigned three times in Italy, conveniently at Milan, Florence, and Genoa; he commanded an army of brigand mercenaries, the worst scourge of the age, in an effort to lose them in Switzerland, his only failure; he picked the right year to revisit England, 1376, the year of John Wycliffe's trial, the Good Parliament, and the deathbed of the Black Prince at which he was present; he was escort for the emperor at all the stage plays, pageantry, and festivities during the imperial visit to Paris; he was chosen for his eloquence and tact to negotiate with the urban rebels of Paris in 1382, and at a truce parley with the English at which a member of the opposite team just happened to be Geoffrey Chaucer; he was agent or envoy to the pope, the duke of Brittany, and other difficult characters in delicate situations; he was a patron and friend of Froissart and owned the oldest surviving copy of the *Chronicle*; his castle was celebrated in a poem by Deschamps; he assisted at the literary competition for the *Cent Ballades* of which his cousin, the Bastard of Coucy, was one of the authors; on the death of his father-in-law, King Edward, he returned his wife *and* the Order of the Garter to England; his daughter was "divorced at Rome by means of false witnesses" by her dissolute husband; he commanded an overseas expedition to Tunisia; he founded a monastery at Soissons; he testified at the canonization process of Pierre de Luxemburg; at age fifty he was challenged to a joust (in a letter that survives), by the earl of Nottingham, Earl Marshal of England, twenty-three years old, as the person most fitting to confer "honor, valor, chivalry and great renown" on a young knight (though from what I can gather Coucy was too busy to bother with him); he was of course in the king's company at the sensational mad scene when Charles VI went out of his mind, and at the macabre "dance of the savages" afterwards; it was his physician who attended the king and who later ordered his own tomb effigy as a skeleton, the first of its kind in the cult of death; finally, as "the most experienced and skillful of all the knights of France," he was a leader of the last Crusade, and on the way to death met the only medieval experience so far missing from his record—an attested miracle. In short, he supplies leads to every subject—marriage and divorce, religion, insurrection, literature, Italy, England, war, politics, and a wonderful range of the most interesting people of his time, from pope to peasant. Among them, I may have rather reached for Catherine of Siena, but almost everyone else in the book actually at some point crossed paths with Coucy.

Once having decided upon him, the more I found out while pursuing his traces through the chronicles and genealogies, the more he offered. The study of his tempestuous dynasty dating back to the tenth century, with the adventures in law, war, and love of his ungovernable, not to say ferocious forebears, made in itself a perfect prism of the earlier Middle Ages, which I needed for background. When I came upon the strange and marvelous ceremony of the *Rissoles* performed each year in the courtyard of Coucy-le-chateau, with its strands reaching back into a tangle of pagan, barbarian, feudal, and Christian sources, I knew that there in front of me was medieval society in microcosm and, as I wrote in the book, the many-layered elements of Western man.

As Coucy was a find, so for America at the turn of the twentieth century was Speaker Reed, or Czar Reed as he was called. As soon as I discovered this independent and uncompromising monument of a man, I knew I had what I wanted for the American chapter in *The Proud Tower*, a book about the forces at work in society in the last years before 1914. He was so obviously "writable"—if I may invent a word, which is against my principles—that I could not believe that, except for a routine political biography published in 1914 and an uninspired academic study in 1930, nothing had been written about him since his death in 1902. I now felt he was my personal property and became seized by the fear that someone else would surely see his possibilities and publish something in the years before my book—of which he formed only one part in eight—could appear. Novelists, I suppose, are free of this fear, but it haunts the rest of us from the moment we have found an exciting and hitherto untreated subject. Unbelievably, as it seemed to me, Reed remained invisible to others, and as soon as I had written the chapter I took the precaution of arranging with *American Heritage* to publish it separately a year before the book as a whole was completed.

Reed was an ideal focus, not least because, as an anti-Imperialist, he represented the losers of that era in our history. Usually, it is the winners who capture the history books. We all know about Manifest Destiny and McKinley and Teddy Roosevelt and Admiral Mahan, but it is astonishing how much more dramatic an issue becomes if the opponents'—in this case the anti-Imperialists'—views are given equal play, and the contest is told as if the outcome were still in the balance.

Though the events of the chapter are confined to less than a decade, I learned more about the ideas that formed our country than I had in all my years since first grade. Reed led, through the anti-Imperialist cause, to Samuel Gompers, E.L. Godkin, Charles Eliot Norton, William James, Charles William Eliot (and what a writable character he was!), Carl Schurz, Andrew Carnegie, Moorfield Storey, and to their attitudes and beliefs about America. All America's traditions were reflected there. Our development up to that time and, indeed since, was caught in the prism of the struggle over expansion.

In form, the piece on Reed is a biographical sketch, which is a distinct form of its own with a long literary history. As a rule such sketches are grouped in a collective volume, often by the dozen, like eggs: *The Twelve Caesars, Twelve Against the*

Gods, Twelve Bad Men, and others. The advantage of the form is that one can extract the essence—the charm or drama, the historical or philosophical or other meaning—of the subject's life without having to follow him through all the callow years, the wrong turnings, and the periods in every life of no particular significance. Reed was an excellent choice for many reasons: because of his outsize and memorable appearance— he was a physical giant six foot three inches tall, weighing 300 pounds, always dressed completely in black, with a huge clean-shaven face like a casaba melon; and, because of his quotable wit, his imposing character, his moral passion, and the tragic irony linking the two great contests of his life—one over the Silent Quorum and the other over the treaty assuming sovereignty over the Philippines. The first in its mad action was a writer's dream, and the second brought into focus the struggle of ideas at the turn of the century that marked the change from the old America to the new.

The Silent Quorum was a custom by which minority members of the House could defeat any legislation they did not like by refusing to answer "present" when called to establish a quorum for the vote. As Republican Speaker of the House, Reed had made up his mind to end once and for all the device that made a mockery of the congressional process. He succeeded in scenes, as a reporter wrote, "of such wild excitement, burning indignation, scathing denunciation and really dangerous conditions" as had never before been witnessed on the floor. Pandemonium reigned, the Democrats foamed with rage, a hundred of them were on their feet at once howling for recognition. One represen-tative, a diminutive former Confederate cavalry general, unable to reach the front because of the crowded aisles, came down from the rear, "leaping from desk to desk as an ibex leaps from crag to crag." The only Democrat not on his feet at this point was a huge representative from Texas who sat in his seat significantly whetting a bowie knife on his boot.

Recalling that scene here is for me simply self-indulgence; I had such fun writing it. In the end after five days of furious battle, Reed triumphed and succeeded in imposing a new set of voting rules that ensured that the will of the majority would thereafter govern. It was a long stride, as he said, in the direction of responsible government. Five years later, when it came to a vote on the annexation of Hawaii and subsequently, on the treaty taking over the Philippines (which Reed as an anti-Imperialist bitterly opposed), the purpose of the Quorum battle came to a test with inescapable moral fate, against himself. Still Speaker, he might—by summoning all his authority and manipulating every parliamentary wile of which he was the master—have stifled the vote, but if he did he would nullify the reform he had earlier won. He had to choose between his hatred of foreign conquest and his own rules. Knowing too well the value of what he had accomplished, he could make only one choice. His victory over the Silent Quorum gave the victory to the expansionist sentiment he despised.

To me it seemed a drama of classic shape and I have always thought it would make a good play if only some perceptive playwright would come forward to write it. None has, I suspect because the playwrights of today prefer to find tragedy in the lives of little people, in pale Laura and her glass menagerie, in the death of a salesman, in loneliness crying for little Sheba to come back. Something about our time does not like the great—though doubtless pathos and frustration are as true for humanity as the theme of *The Trojan Women.*

Another find for *The Proud Tower* was Richard Strauss, who served as a prism for a view of Imperial Germany on the eve of 1914. I did not want to do the usual portrayal of Wilhelmine Germany in terms of Wilhelm II and the militarists and the Agadir Crisis and all that. The business of rewriting what is already well known holds no charm for me. I would find no stimulus to write unless I were learning something new and telling the reader something new, in content or in form. I have never understood how the English manage to interest themselves in turning out all those lives of Queen Victoria, Wellington, Cromwell, Mary Queen of Scots—the large and the hackneyed. For the writer, plowing through the material for such a book must be like sitting down every day to a meal of cream of wheat: no surprises.

The choice of Strauss, which meant writing familiarly of music, of which I have no special knowledge, seemed almost too challenging. The reason for it was that, since I knew myself to be frankly prejudiced against Germans, I thought that both for me and the reader it would be fresh and interesting to approach them through the best they had to offer rather than the worst; through the arts, rather than through militarism, and through the one art in which they excelled—music. The result was that I enjoyed myself. Strauss proved satisfactorily Teutonic, and his wife, with her fanatic housekeeping and screams of wrath, even more so. Like Coucy, Strauss led everywhere: through his *Zarathustra* to Nietzsche, a key to the period; through his *Salome* to fin-de-siècle decadence; through conductorship of the Berlin Opera to Berlin and the beer gardens and German society and the Sieges Allee with its glittering marble rows of helmeted Hohenzollerns in triumphant attitudes; to Wilhelm II in his fancy as "an art-loving prince"; to Vienna through Strauss's collaborator von Hofmannsthal; to the brilliant explosion, as the new century opened, of Diaghilev's Russian Ballet, of the Fauves led by Matisse, the dance of Isadora Duncan, the sculpture of Rodin, the *Rites of Spring* of Stravinsky, the scandal of Nijinsky's performance as Debussy's Faun, and to all the frenzy and fecundity of that feverish eleventh hour that was seeking to express itself in emotion and art. I did not have to labor Strauss to carry out the theme; it was all in Romain Rolland's uncanny prophecy after hearing Strauss conduct *Zarathustra*: "Aha! Germany as the all-powerful will not keep her balance for long. Nietzsche, Strauss, the Kaiser—Neroism is in the air!" Equally perceptive, the Austrian critic Herman Bahr heard in Strauss's *Elektra* "a pride born of limitless power," a defiance of order "lured back toward chaos." Thus is biography welded to history.

The life of "Vinegar Joe" Stilwell was the nearest I have come to a formal biography, although I conceived of it from the start as a vehicle to carry the larger subject of the American experience in China. Stilwell was not a lucky find like Coucy; he was the natural and obvious choice. His career had been connected with China throughout the period of the modern Sino-American relationship from 1911, the year of the Chinese Revolution, to the penultimate year of World War II when he was the commanding American in the China Theater. He represented, as I believe, the best that America has tried to do in Asia, and he was in himself a representative American, yet sufficiently nontypical to be a distinct and memorable individual. The peculiar thing about him is that he left a different impression on different readers; some came away from the book admiring, and others rather disliking him, which only proves what every writer knows: that a certain number of readers will always find in one's book not what one has written, but what they bring to it.

Or it may be that I failed with Stilwell to achieve a firm characterization, which may reflect a certain ambivalence. I certainly admired him, and critics have said that I was, indeed, too energetically his champion. Yet I was never sure that I would have actually liked him in real life, or that he, to put it mildly, would have approved of me. Perhaps it is fortunate that, although I passed through Peking in 1935 when he was there as military attaché, we never met.

This raises the question: Who is the ideal biographer? One who has known his subject or one who has not? Boswell, I suppose, is generally credited with the most perfect biography ever written (or rather, personal memoir, for it was not really a biography), and the other biographies that stand out over the ages are mostly those written by friends, relatives, or colleagues of the subject: Joinville's *Memoirs of*

Saint Louis; Comine's *Memoirs of Louis XI*; the three monuments by sons-in-law—Tacitus's *Life of Agricola*, William Roper's *Sir Thomas More*, John Lockhart's *Life of Sir Walter Scott*; Lincoln by his two secretaries, John Nicolay and John Hay; Gladstone by his colleague Lord Morley; and, in our time, Doris Kearns's *L.B.J.*

Such biographers have a unique intimacy, and if in addition they are reasonably honest and perceptive, they can construct a life that those of us not acquainted with, or not contemporary with our subject can never match. If the contemporary biographer is blessed with Boswell's genius as reporter and writer, the result may be supreme. On the other hand, he may distort, consciously or unconsciously, through access to too much information, and produce a warehouse instead of a portrait. Lockhart's work fills 4,000 pages in nine volumes; Nicolay and Hay's about the same in ten volumes. Unfortunately, in the matter of superabundance, the secondary biographer of today is not far behind.

In time and intimacy, the most immediate life is, of course, autobiography or diaries, letters and autobiographical memoirs. These are the primary stuff of history: the *Confessions* of St. Augustine and of Jean Jacques Rousseau; Pepys's *Diary*; Ben Franklin's *Autobiography*; the *Memoirs* of St. Simon; the letters of the Marquise de Sevigné; the journals of John Evelyn, Charles Greville, and the Goncourt brothers; the *Apologia* of Cardinal Newman; and, I suppose I must add, that acme of self-conscious enterprise, the *Education of Henry Adams*. Even when tendentious or lying these works are invaluable, but they are in a different category than biography in the sense that concerns us here.

When one tries to think of who the great secondary biographers are, no peaks stand out like the primaries. There are, of course, the four Gospels of Matthew, Mark, Luke, and John, who closely followed but were not acquainted with their subject. Although they tell us what we know of the life of Jesus, their motive was not so much biographical as propagandistic—a spreading of the gospel (which means good news) that the Messiah had come. Since then one may pick one's own choice: Carlyle's *Cromwell*, perhaps, Amy Kelly's *Eleanor of Aquitaine,* Sam Morison's *Christopher Columbus,* Cecil Woodham-Smith's *Florence Nightingale,* Leon Edel's *Henry James,* Justin Kaplan's *Mark Twain* and *Steffens.* With apologies to them, however, I think the primary biographers still have the edge.

I shall never be among them because it seems to me that the historian—whether or not the biographer—needs distance. It has once or twice been proposed to me that I write a biography of my grandfather, Henry Morgenthau, Sr., a man of great charm and accomplishment, but though I loved and revered him, I shrink from the very idea. Love and reverence are not the proper mood for an historian. I have written one short piece on a particular aspect of his life, but I could never do more.

In the subjects I have used I am not personally involved. The nearest I came was in the course of working on the Stilwell papers, then housed in Mrs. Stilwell's home in Carmel, when I became friendly with members of the family who were, and are, very nice people and, I am happy to say, have remained my friends even *after* publication. Friendly relations, I have to acknowledge, inevitably exerted a certain unspoken restraint on writing anything nasty about the deceased general, had I been so inclined. However, I cannot think of anything I really toned down, except possibly the foul language to be found in Stilwell's diary. Restraint in that case, however, was less concerned with the family's sensibilities than with my own. Not having been brought up with four-letter words and explicit scatalogical images, I found it impossible to bring myself to repeat them, and yet to omit what I then took to be an indication of character violated my conscience as an historian. I eventually worked around that problem by a generalized, if nonspecific reference to Stilwell's vocabulary. Exposed as we have all been since to the polite and delicate language of the last decade, I think now that I took the problem too seriously. I had no idea then how common and banal these words were in male conversation.

More difficult was Stilwell's horrid reference to Roosevelt as "Rubberlegs," which truly shocked me. That he was a normal Roosevelt-hater of the kind in Peter Arno's famous cartoon, "Let's go to the Trans-Lux and hiss Roosevelt," and that he had a talent for inventing wicked nicknames, I knew, but to make fun of a physical infirmity seemed to me unforgivable. In a real agony over whether to include his usage or not, I conducted considerable research among people of Stilwell's vintage into the phenomenon of Roosevelt-hating, and even found an entire book on the subject. It showed that, compared to many things said in those circles, Stilwell's usage was run-of-the mill, so I put it in, though it felt like picking up a cockroach. Though minor, this episode shows how a biographer can become emotionally involved with her subject.

Whether in biography or straight history, my form is narrative because that is what comes naturally to me. I think of history as a story and myself as a storyteller, and the reader as a listener whose attention must be held if he is not to wander away. Schererazade only survived because she managed to keep the sultan absorbed in her tales and wondering what would happen next. While I am not under quite such exigent pressure, I nevertheless want the reader to turn the page and keep on turning to the end. Narrative, if the action is kept moving through every paragraph, has the power to accomplish this. It also has inherent validity: it is the spine of history and the key to causation. Events do not happen in categories—economic, intellectual, military—they happen in sequence. When they are arranged in sequence as strictly as possible down to month, week, and even day, cause and effect that may have been previously obscure, will often become clear, like secret ink.

Sometimes, as in the Middle Ages, the necessary

information to establish sequence is missing, whereas in recent history the problem is more likely to be too much information. If the narrative is to be kept moving, this requires condensing, which is the hardest work I know, and selection, which is the most delicate. Selection is the task of distinguishing the significant from the insignificant; it is the test of the writer as historian and as artist. The governing principle of selection is that it must honestly illustrate and never distort. By the very fact of inclusion or omission the writer has tremendous power to leave an impression that may not in fact be justified. He must, therefore, resist the temptation to use an isolated incident, however colorful, to support a thesis, or by judicious omission to shade the evidence. Whether the historian is a Marxist or moralist, a psychologist or revisionist, is irrelevant. What matters is that he have a conscience and keep it on guard.

Unhappily, biography has lately been overtaken by a school that has abandoned the selective in favor of the all-inclusive. I think this development is part of the anti-excellence spirit of our time that insists on the equality of everything and is thus reduced to the theory that all facts are of equal value and that the biographer or historian should not presume to exercise judgment. To that I can only say, if he cannot exercise judgment, he should not be in the business. A portraitist does not achieve a likeness by giving sleeve buttons and shoelaces equal value to mouth and eyes.

Today in biography we are presented with the subject's life reconstructed day by day from birth to death, including every new dress or pair of pants, every juvenile poem, every journey, every letter, every loan, every accepted or rejected invitation, every telephone message, every drink at every bar. The result is one of those thousand-page heavies in which all the hard work has been left to the reader who can hardly be blamed if he finds the task unrewarding.

Lytton Strachey, the father of modern biography at its most readable, if not most reliable, and an artist to the last pen stroke, would have been horrified to find himself today the subject of one of these laundry-list biographies in two very large volumes. His own motto was "The exclusion of everything that is redundant and nothing that is significant." If that advice is now ignored, Strachey's influence on psychological interpretation, on the other hand, has been followed to excess. In pre-Strachey biographies the inner life, like the two-thirds of an iceberg that is under water, went largely unseen and uninvestigated. Since Strachey, and of course since Freud, the hidden secrets, especially if they are shady, are the biographer's goal and the reader's delight. It is argued—though I am not sure on what ground—that the public has a right to know the underside, and the biographer busies himself in penetrating private crannies and uncovering the failures and delinquencies his subject strove to conceal. Where once biography was devoted to setting up marble statues, it is now devoted, in Andre Maurois' words, to "pulling dead lions by the beard."

A whole book is written to show that Martin Luther was constipated. This may be fascinating to some, but is it, in fact, historically significant? Anyone who has studied John Wycliffe and the Lollard movement of the fourteenth century, and Jan Hus and the Hussite movement of the fifteenth century, knows that by the time Luther came along in the sixteenth, the Protestant breach with Rome was inevitable. If Luther had not pinned up his theses on the church door at Worms, someone else would have done so in Prague or Cologne or London. Luther's anal difficulties may offer the psychologist an interesting field of investigation, but they did not create the Protestant Reformation, and if they did not, then why should they concern us?

Having a strong instinctive sense of privacy myself, I feel no great obligation to pry into a subject's private life, and reveal—unless it is clearly relevant—what he would have wanted to keep private. "What business has the public to know of Byron's wildnesses?" asked Tennyson. "He has given them fine work and they ought to be satisfied." Tennyson had a point. Do we really have to know of some famous person that he wet his pants at age six and practiced oral sex at sixty? I suppose it is quite possible that Shakespeare might have indulged in one or both of these habits. If evidence to that effect were suddenly to be found today, what then would be the truth of Shakespeare—the new finding or *King Lear*? Would the plays interest us more because we had knowledge of the author's excretory or amatory digressions?

No doubt many would unhesitatingly answer "yes" to that question. It seems to me, however, that insofar as biography is used to illumine history, voyeurism has no place. Happily, in the case of the greatest English writer, we know and are likely to know close to nothing about his private life. I like this vacuum, this miracle, this great floating monument of work that has no explanation at all.

Notes on the Contributors

Leon Edel received his doctorate from the University of Paris. His teaching positions include seventeen years at New York University, the last five of which were spent as Henry James Professor of English and American Letters, and six years as Citizens Professor of English at the University of Hawaii. A recipient of Guggenheim and Bollingen fellowships, Mr. Edel was honored with an award for creative writing in biography from the National Institute of Arts and Letters (1959), to which he was later elected; a National Book Award for nonfiction (1963), a Pulitzer Prize for biography (1963), the Gold Medal of the American Academy/Institute of Arts and Letters for biography, and the Hawaii Writer's Award (1978). He is a fellow of the American Academy of Arts and Sciences and the Royal Society of Literature. Best known for his five-volume biography of Henry James, Professor Edel has written *Bloomsbury A House of Lions*, to be published this year. He is editing the journals of Edmund Wilson and further letters of Henry James.

Justin Kaplan's *Mr. Clemens and Mark Twain* won the National Book Award in Arts and Letters and the Pulitzer Prize for biography in 1967. He is also the author of *Lincoln Steffens* (1974), *Mark Twain and His World* (1974), and a forthcoming biography of Walt Whitman.

Alfred Kazin was the literary editor of *The New Republic* from 1942-43 and contributing editor from 1943-45. Thereafter he held fellowships from the Rockefeller and the Guggenheim Foundations. Professor Kazin has taught at Harvard, Amherst, Berkeley, and New York State University at Stony Brook. A Distinguished Professor of English at the City University of New York graduate school and Hunter College, he was, in 1978-79, William White Professor of English at Notre Dame. His books include: *On Native Grounds* (1942) and his autobiographical trilogy: *A Walker in the City* (1951), *Starting Out in the Thirties* (1965), and *New York Jew* (1978).

Doris Kearns taught at Harvard—where she received her Ph.D. in government—from 1969-77, and has been a trustee of her alma mater, Colby College, Wesleyan University, and the Robert F. Kennedy Foundation. As a White House Fellow, she served as a special assistant to Secretary of Labor Willard Wirtz in 1967 and became special assistant to President Lyndon Johnson in the following year. From 1969-73 she was a special consultant to the former president. Her biography, *Lyndon Johnson and the American Dream*, was published in 1976. She has also done sportswriting and is currently at work on a book concerning three generations of the Kennedy family.

M arc Pachter graduated from the University of California at Berkeley with great distinction in 1964. Thereafter he was a Woodrow Wilson Fellow and a Five Year Prize Fellow in American History at Harvard University, where he taught in the honors program. He edited *Abroad in America: Visitors to the New Nation, 1776-1914* (1976), and has written *A Gallery of Presidents*, to be published this year, and articles for the *Dictionary of American Biography*. He has lectured for the New York Historical Society, the Williamsburg Antiques Forum, throughout the United States for the Smithsonian Institution, and in Spain, France, Romania, Sweden, Norway, and Denmark for the United States Information Agency. Since 1974, Mr. Pachter has served as the historian of the National Portrait Gallery, Smithsonian Institution.

T heodore Rosengarten graduated from Amherst College in 1966 and received his Ph.D. from Harvard University. He was awarded an Ethnic Studies grant by the Ford Foundation for 1972-73. His book, *All God's Dangers: The Life of Nate Shaw* won the National Book Award in Contemporary Affairs for 1974. Mr. Rosengarten lives in McClellanville, South Carolina.

B arbara W. Tuchman began her career as a staff member of the Institute of Pacific Relations in 1934-35, and then of *The Nation* in 1936-38, serving on the Far East desk of the Office of War Information during World War II. She is the author of six works of history that have been translated into fourteen languages and have won two Pulitzer Prizes—for *The Guns of August* (1962) and *Stilwell and the American Experience in China* (1971). Her other books are *Bible and Sword* (1956), *The Zimmermann Telegram* (1958), *The Proud Tower* (1966), *Notes from*

China, (a collection of articles, 1972), and *A Distant Mirror* (1978). Mrs. Tuchman received her bachelor's degree from Radcliffe College in 1933 and has been awarded the honorary doctorate of Letters from Columbia, Yale, and nine other institutions. In 1978 she won the Gold Medal for History of the American Academy/Institute of Arts and Letters. She has contributed to *Foreign Affairs, The Atlantic Monthly, Harper's, New York Times,* and other journals, and delivered the Phi Beta Kappa address at Harvard in 1963 and the Charter Day address at the University of California, Berkeley, in 1974. She was elected president of the American Academy/Institute of Arts and Letters in January 1979.

Geoffrey Wolff, a *summa cum laude* graduate of Princeton University, was a Fulbright Scholar at Cambridge University. He has taught at Princeton and Istanbul University and is now Adjunct Associate Professor of Literature at Middlebury College and book critic at *Esquire.* A Senior Fellow of the National Endowment for the Humanities and twice a Guggenheim Fellow, Wolff is the author of three novels and of *Black Sun,* a biography of Harry Crosby, published in 1976. His memory of his father, *The Duke of Deception,* will be published this year.